Giovanna Magi

ART AND HISTORY

LUXOR

KARNAK - THE VALLEY OF THE KINGS

BONECHI

Publication created and designed by Casa Editrice Bonechi

Editorial management: Giovanna Magi

Graphic design: Sonia Gottardo. *Graphics, Make-up:* Manuela Ranfagni
Cover: Laura Settesoldi. *Editing:* Anna Baldini. *Drawings:* Stefano Benini

Texts and picture research: Giovanna Magi
Translation by Paula Boomsliter

Printed in Italy by Centro Stampa Editoriale Bonechi - Sesto Fiorentino

The majority of the photographs are property of the Casa Editrice Bonechi *Archives. They were taken by*
Paolo Giambone, Luigi di Giovine, Marco Carpi Ceci, Andrea Pistolesi, Emanuela Crimini, Michael Clears.

The photographs and text relative to the Tomb of Nefertari and the Tomb of Pashed, and the photograph on page 119, bottom, were used with the kind permission of the author Mario Tosi.

The publisher would like to thank Dr. Mario Tosi for his invaluable assistance.

Other photographs were provided by
Archivio Scala: *page 3*
Gianni Dagli Orti: *pages 13, 23 below left, 45 above left and center, 49 above, 50 below, 51 above and center, 56, 58, 59, 60, 61, 62 center and below right, 63 below left, 66, 67, 68, 70, 71, 72, 74, 75, 76 below, 112, 113 below, 118 above, 119 above, 130 above, 136 above, 137 below, 153 below, 154 above.*

Arte e Storia · Luxor - n° 39 - Pubblicazione Periodica Trimestrale - Autorizzazione del Tribunale di Firenze n° 3873 del 4/8/1989 Direttore Responsabile: Giovanna Magi

* * *

FROM THEBES TO LUXOR

A strip of green in the midst of yellow desert, cultivated fields, and a background of red rocks - the Libyan Chain - are the setting for Luxor, once, together with the area of Karnak, one of the greatest capitals of the ancient world. And it is still a captivating city, with its modern hotels lining the banks of the Nile, the feluccas gliding over the tranquil waters of the river, and the small silent streets of the bazaar coming to life towards evening with colors, sounds, and lights.

This is the ancient, great city of Thebes, capital of the Egyptian empire for almost a thousand years, called by Homer in the ninth canto of the Iliad "the hundred-gated Thebes," within "only the grains of sand of the desert surpassed the quantity of riches enclosed within" its walls. The Copts called it Tapé, hence the Greek Thebai, and our Thebes - but for the Egyptians it was Uaset, "the dominant," and Niut, "the City;" later, it was only naturally called Diospolis Magna. Its present name, Luxor, derives from the Arabic Al-Uqsur, a translation of the Latin castra - in fact, the Romans maintained two encampments in the city.

In the Memphite period, it was a small village, site of worship of the war god Munt, whose temples marked the boundaries of the territory. In the 10th century, its importance grew thanks to its geographical position and for political reasons, and the military successes of its princes eventually succeeded in making it a power. Thebes reached the height of its glory during the New Kingdom: the Thebans defeated the Hyksos invaders with to the intercession of the great god Amon, who thus became the god of the realm and was worshiped in the triad with Mut and Khonsu. This was the era of the great victories and triumphs in Anterior Asia, in Nubia, and in Libya. It was perhaps the most felicitous of periods in Egyptian history and Thebes had no rivals: the victorious pharaohs accumulated incredible wealth ("city where the houses are rich treasuries") in spoils from the wars; merchants arrived from the Red Sea, the Persian Gulf, and even from the Sahara, via the oases routes, to make their fortunes - and those of the inhabitants of Thebes, who, it is said, reached the incredible number of half a million in that period.

The temples, the dwellings of the gods, rose on the east bank of the river; buildings for the cult of the dead sovereigns rose on the west bank. Beyond this row of temples, running parallel to the river, is the imposing rock bluff which hides the Valley of the Kings. Then, inexorable for Thebes as for other cities, the decline. The geographical position that a thousand years earlier had favored its rise to power now became the prime factor in its decadence: too far from the "hot" zone of the Delta, where the Ramessides were forced to create military posts to stem the foreign invasions, Thebes lost its political, spiritual, and military

A large painting by Giuseppe Angelelli, in the Archaeological Museum of Florence, of all the members of the French-Tuscan expedition of Champollion-Rosellini, which traveled up the Nile Valley to Wadi Halfa and stopped in Thebes from March to September 1829. Jean-François Champollion, the decipherer of the Egyptian hieroglyphics, is dressed in Eastern garb and is seated at the center of the group. To his right stands Ippolito Rosellini, Professor of Oriental Languages at the University of Pisa and founder of Egyptology in Italy, portrayed in the act of drawing. The painters Cherubini, Angelelli, Duchesne, Bertin, and Lehoux, the draftsman Nestor L'Hote, the archaeologist Lenormant, the engineer Gaetano Rosellini, the Sienese physician Alessandro Ricci, and the naturalists Giuseppe Raddi and Felice Galastri also took part in the expedition.

Hector Horeau's imaginary reconstruction of Thebes. From the top of a pylon, the viewer's eye sweeps over Karnak and its sumptuous monumental complex: the homes of the priests immersed in gardens, the entrance pylons, the long sphinx-lined avenue leading to the Temple of Luxor. On the left, some period objects as imagined by Horeau: rugs, seats, pots for cooling water, and containers for papyri.

supremacy. The dynasties that followed came from the Delta, and the cities of Tanis, Bubastis, and Sais took Thebes' place as capital of Egypt.

Left defenseless, Thebes was easy prey for all and sundry: the Assyrian invasions of the 7th century, at the hand first of Esarhaddon and then of Ashurbanipal, were devastating: the inhabitants were deported as slaves, the statues and the treasuries were sacked, the temples were destroyed. By the Ptolemaic era, Thebes had become a provincial backwater.

Following an attempted rebellion under Ptolemy IX Soter II and an insurrection against the Roman yoke, the city was razed by Cornelius Gallus. In 27 BC, a terrible earthquake fended the coup de grace to the entire region.

As Christianity spread, the sacred significance of the temples of the Egyptian gods and the tombs of the pharaohs was obfuscated as homes, sheds, and barns were built over or abutting them. But as Thebes slowly (and literally) disappeared, Luxor took its place.

From Pompey's column in Alexandria, past the pyramids of Giza and Saqqarah, through Thebes and Medinet Habu to the Temple of Abu Simbel. Thus, with no concern for real distances in a breathtaking fantastical flight, Hector Horeau illustrates the valley of the Nile. This plate is part of the book *Panorama d'Egypte et de Nubes* published in Paris in 1841.

The rise and expansion of tourism in Luxor has had substantial consequences for the hotel trade. The number of accommodations has increased greatly during the past few decades, but amidst the modern buildings of the most important European hotel chains, the charm of the Winter Palace, with its austere architecture, its thick carpets, and its terraces opening on the sights and sounds of the river, still remains unequaled. The many souvenir shops that have opened near the hotel have detracted nothing from the atmosphere of enchantment and glamour that still lingers in the magnificent salons and the shady gardens that stretch out behind the building. Archeologists, journalists, writers, politicians, members of world high society: leafing through the guest register of this hotel is a little like reading the history of old Europe as its protagonists stopped along the banks of the Nile to dip into Egypt's thousands of years of history.

During the 1800s, Luxor was a tranquil, laborious village of Upper Egypt that drowsed peacefully while great political and social events played out in Cairo and Suez.
After 1811, when Thomas Cook opened the world's first travel agency, all of Egypt rapidly began to open its doors to the new tourist industry.
Luxor, with its fascinating ruins, docks for the dahabieh on the riverfront, and its climate, so mild in comparison to the European winters, soon became a vacation spot for the new tourists, the winter residence of rich Englishmen, and a compulsory stopover during the long voyages made by European officials.
Luxor, with its palaces and the mysterious Valley that ran along the other side of the river, soon also attracted many archaeologists, writers, and painters, who flocked to study, document, and describe all that was still visible of the glorious past of Thebes or to discover what of it was still hidden in the sands. There thus arrived Jean-François Champollion and Ippolito Rosellini, Heinrich and Emil Brugsch, and Lady Lucy Duff-Gordon, who lived for seven years in a house built on the roof of the Temple of Amon.
Luxor also attracted another category of visitors: the improvised archaeologists, the seekers of antiques and treasure, the collectors - with no scruples but lots of money - and the tomb raiders, every ready to kill or betray for a handful of piasters. And with them was born the black market for antiques, with its authentic finds and its junk, its real treasures and blatant fakes.
All these people, whose stories were often strangely intertwined, helped penetrate the thick veils of mystery that still surrounded ancient Egyptian civilization.
Luxor, constantly expanding, with more and more modern hotels, became one of Egypt's most important historical and archeological tourism draws.

David Roberts and Hector Horeau - Two 19th-Century "Tourists"

Throughout the 19th century, a great number English, French, and German artists
attempted to transmit to the West - with their words, impressions, sketches, and
drawings - the charm and fascination of Egypt. David Roberts and Hector Horeau, the
first a Scotsman, the second French, each approached Egyptian civilization from the
standpoint of his own particular style, technique, and personality - but both were
overwhelmed by the emotions felt by practically any Western visitor to this land: intense
curiosity and wonderment.
David Roberts, who spent eleven months traveling through Egypt, Syria, and the Holy Land,

was wont to return a monument many times during the same day to capture the subtle nuances of the light as it changed with the passage of the hours; David Roberts, the son of an Edinburgh shoemaker and later member of the Royal Academy; David Roberts, an honored guest at Queen Victoria's court on several occasions. And Hector Horeau, who sailed from Cairo on a modest boat that cost him 150 francs a month; Hector Horeau, who dressed in Turkish garb in order to show respect for local customs as he plied his way up the Nile to Abu Simbel; Hector Horeau, who wrote "I left alone, with no companions except a manservant, more a master in my boat than a king in his kingdom." Luxor, Karnak, the Valley of the Kings, the Colossi of Memnon . . . rendered with an eye to the monument and one to the colorful, tattered humanity that populated the ruins of the temples or loitered lazily on the feluccas that slipped along the river. The message transmitted by the art of David Roberts and Hector Horeau is not one of glory and power: it is rather a deeply touching, whispered homage to a world past, caught on paper and tied with the fine thread of compassionate remembrance.

The Temple of Amon-Ra at Luxor. Views from the river and of the entrance pylon, by Hector Horeau (p. 6, bottom; p. 7, top) and David Roberts. Both artists saw and painted only one of the two obelisks of Ramses II, because by the time they visited Egypt its "twin" had already been shipped off to Paris.

TEMPLE OF AMON-RA

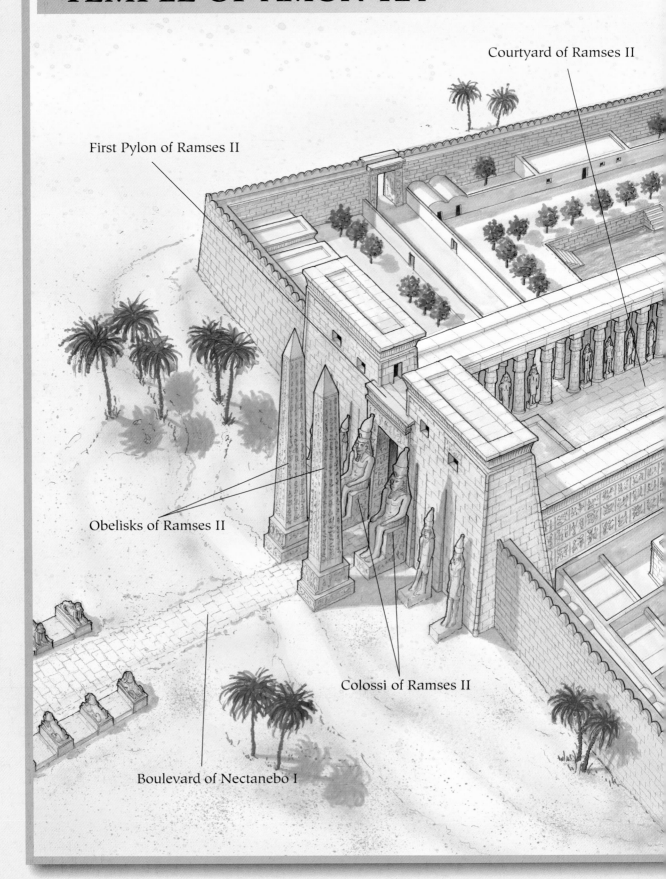

Courtyard of Ramses II

First Pylon of Ramses II

Obelisks of Ramses II

Colossi of Ramses II

Boulevard of Nectanebo I

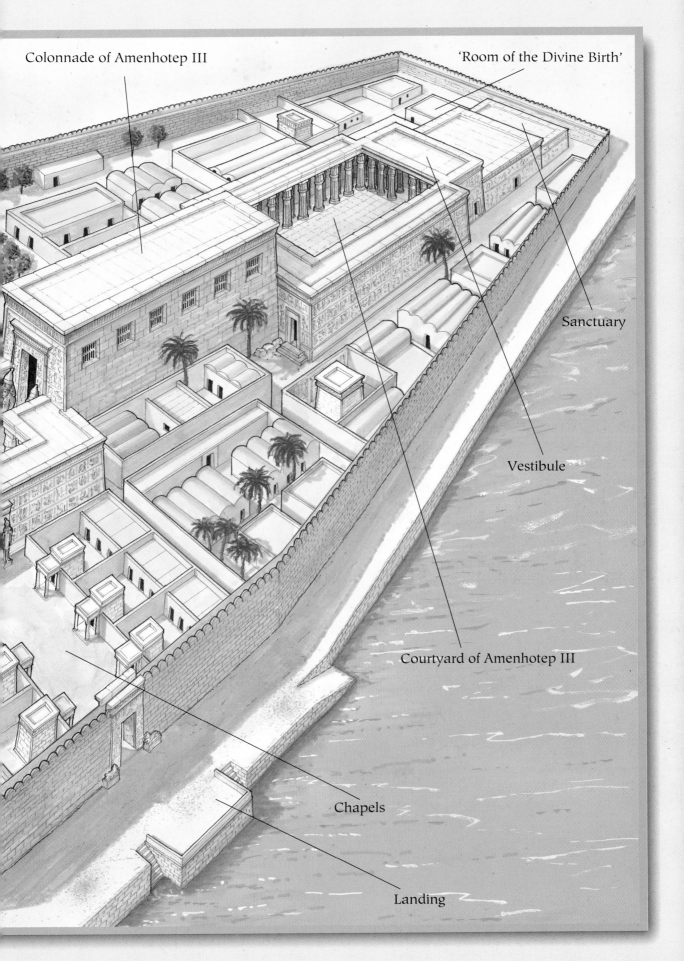

Colonnade of Amenhotep III

'Room of the Divine Birth'

Sanctuary

Vestibule

Courtyard of Amenhotep III

Chapels

Landing

9

THE TEMPLE OF AMON-RA IN LUXOR

The only witness, in Luxor, to its glorious past is the temple built by the ancient Egyptians to the glory of Amon-Ra, king of the gods, and which they called by the name of Southern Harem of Amon. The temple, uncovered in 1883 by Gaston Maspero, is 260 meters long and was mostly built by two pharaohs, Amenhotep III, who began it in the 14th century BC, and Ramses II, who completed it by adding the great porticoed court with its axis shifted eastwards.

Numerous other sovereigns, including Tutankhamen, Horemheb and Alexander the Great, enriched the construction with reliefs, inscriptions and minor buildings.

The Temple of Luxor was joined to that of Karnak by a long dromos or processional avenue paved in stone and flanked by human-headed sphinxes. This street has not yet been completely brought to

light and work is still going on. The avenue ended at the entrance to the Temple of Luxor, at the Great **Pylon** built by Ramses II. Its 65-meter facade is decorated with **bas-reliefs** of scenes from the pharaoh's military campaigns against the Hittites. On the left side are the *Egyptian Camp* and the *War Council*; on the right side, the *Battle of Kadesh*.

The dromos or processional avenue of sphinxes standing before the entrance pylon to the Temple of Amon-Ra is the work of Nectanebo I, a pharaoh of the 30th Dynasty. In Egyptian symbolism, the sphinx was the protector of temples.

At the entrance to the Temple of Amon-Ra are two colossal statues of the seated Ramses II. David Roberts painted them when they were still semi-submerged by the sand, their faces ruined.
On the side of the pedestal is a symbolic scene representing the unification of Upper and Lower Egypt.

Below, in vertical bands of inscribed hieroglyphics, is the so-called *Poem of Pentaur*, which celebrates the pharaoh's courage. The four large vertical slits on the facade were meant to hold flagstaffs.

Originally, the **Great Pylon** was preceded by two obelisks, two seated colossi, and four standing colossi. Today, only the left obelisk, 25 meters high, is still standing: its "twin" was taken to Paris in 1833 and erected by the engineer Jean-Baptiste Apollinaire Lebas in Place de la Concorde on 25 October 1836.

The two granite **colossi**, fifteen and a half meters high on bases about a meter high, represent the pharaoh seated on a throne. Of the other four **pink granite statues** set against the pylon, one represented the queen Nefertari and

The remaining obelisk and the colossi of Ramses II as they are today and as David Roberts saw them, buried up to the chest and, as he remarked, sadly disfigured as was everything in reach of a hammer.

The serenely smiling face of the pharaoh Ramses II in a monumental portrait.

another, on the right and in poor condition, her daughter Merit-Amon.

To the left of the obelisk is a **head of Ramses II**, belonging to one of the colossi in front of the pylon. The triumphal entrance leads into the **Courtyard of Ramses II**, with its double row of columns with closed papyrus capitals and statues in the intercolumnar spaces. On the northwest side of the courtyard is the shrine/depository of the sacred barks. It was built by Thutmose III and dedicated to the triad of Amon, Mut and Khonsu. Commemorative inscriptions and scenes of sacrifices and religious ceremonies decorate the inner walls of the court. From the left, personifications of the mining districts bearing tributes to the god, Ramses II sacrificing to the goddess Seshat, and

the inauguration ceremony of the monumental entrance with the pharaoh's children, bearing flowers, at the head of the procession. The **second pylon** is the formidable back wall erected by Amenhotep III; it was the original entrance to the temple.

It is followed by a 52-meter **colonnade** of two rows of seven campaniform columns, also the work of Amenhotep III, to which the decorations, lively depictions of the great Opet with the procession of sacred barks being carried to Luxor from Karnak and vice versa, were added later by Tutankhamen and Horemheb. The Opet, or Festival of the New Year, lasted somewhat over fifteen days, beginning on the nineteenth day of the second month of the inundation; that is, in late August.

A Souvenir of Egypt

*I*t would seem that, as Napoleon was leaving for his expedition to Egypt in 1798, his wife Joséphine wished him a good trip and asked him to bring her a "small obelisk" as a souvenir. The obelisk that now stands in Paris is anything but small, and Napoleon did not bring it to France. It was Champollion who later requested of the Viceroy of Egypt, Mohammed Ali, that the country give the obelisk as a gift to France's king Louis-Philippe - and received his wish. Following extensive negotiations and a just-as-difficult voyage aboard Le Louxor, the obelisk reached Paris on 23 December 1833. Place de la Concorde was prepared to plans by the architect Lebas, and with a crowd of 200,000 amazed and dumbfounded Parisians attending, the obelisk of Ramses II took its place at the center of the square three years later.

The raising of the obelisk of Luxor in Place de la Concorde on 25 October 1836, in a detail of a painting by F. Dubois (1790-1871) in Paris' Musée Carnavalet.

The architecture of the colonnades of the Temple of Luxor is highly varied, including as it does columns with closed papyrus capitals (above), columns with open papyrus capitals (left), and bundle columns with closed capitals (below).

The ceremony reached its climax when the sacred bark of Amon-Ra, followed by those of Mut and of Khonsu, was carried by thirty priests out of the Temple of Karnak and along the entire avenue of sphinxes to the Temple of Luxor: here the barks were closed in the sanctuary for several days, after which they were accompanied back to the Temple of Karnak by a festive crowd intoning songs and performing sacred dances. At the beginning of the colonnade are two fine **limestone groups** of the pharaoh and a queen. The colonnade gives access to the second courtyard, or **Court of Amenhotep III**, lined on three sides by double rows of bundle columns with closed papyrus capitals.

The fourth side is actually a transversely-placed **hypostyle hall** with four rows of eight columns each, of the same type as those in the courtyard: a true petrified forest of great effect. Next is the **vestibule**, flanked by two rooms; the one on the left is consecrated to Mut, the one on the right, divided in two, to Khonsu and Amon-Min (in Luxor, Amon had taken the form of the ithyphallic Min).

The pharaoh wears the nemes headdress; from his forehead rises the uraeus, the portrayal of the goddess Uadjet, who, in the form of a cobra, protected the king.

The red crown (desheret) was the symbol of Lower Egypt, the white crown (hedjet) of Upper Egypt. Superposition of the two diadems created the double crown (pschent), symbol of the unified kingdoms.

The system of hieroglyphics, which perhaps originated in the predynastic period, included about 800 signs. The names of the pharaohs were enclosed in an oval or oblong figure called a cartouche: when he set out to decipher the Rosetta Stone, Champollion began his work from the names of Cleopatra and Ptolemy inscribed in their cartouches.

The coronation name of Ramses II was User-ma'at-ra Setep-en-ra, meaning "Bountiful in his Justice is Ra, Chosen of Ra."

The first courtyard of Ramses II, closed off on the north side by the small Temple of Thutmose III dedicated to the Theban triad of Amon, Mut, and Khonsu.

The courtyard of Ramses II, with the Osiris statues of the pharaoh in the spaces between the columns.

Pierre Loti, the Chronicler of the Orient

Louis-Marie-Julien Viaud is certainly better known by the pseudonym under which he published his travel books: Pierre Loti. Pierre Loti wrote among the ruins of the Egyptian temples and on the blazing sands of Nubia, but he was always most fascinated by the hypnotic Thebes, whose decline as a result of the Westernizing influences the English inevitably bring with them he felt to be inevitable. Inside the Temple of Amon-Ra, Loti was able, for a brief moment, to forget Luxor, the noise of the river craft, the interfering clerks of the Cook Agency, and the plaster and cement of the bulky Winter Palace, and to rediscover the great and eternal Thebes. Loti stood in silent wonder before the

statue of Ramses II, overpowered by the majesty of those colossi that surrounded him, and wrote of their "proud bearing, one leg forward as though to begin a march that no force on Earth could check." The three Ramses' stand challenging time, " . . . their heads high, smiling . . . as they stride confidently into eternity."

Next is the offering room, with four columns and decorated with scenes of religious ceremonies in which Amenhotep appears; then the sanctuary, or depository of the sacred barks, which was transformed into a chapel running along the axis of the temple by Alexander the Great, who appears in the presence of Amon in the inner and outer wall decorations.

The colonnades of the courtyard of Amenhotep III differ in the style of the capitals, which may be open or closed papyrus flowers. The barrels of the columns also differ, being either smooth or bundled.

Two limestone sculptural groups of Ramses II, alone and with the mutilated statue of a queen.

A detail of the great hypostyle courtyard of Amenhotep III: the "Chief of All Works" was the architect Amenhotep son of Hapu, who was later elevated to the status of deity.

Other rooms open off around the sanctuary, like the interesting **Birth Room** with relief decorations chronicling the divine conception and birth of the king: Amon speaking with Thoth, with the pharaoh, and with the queen; Khnum fashioning two new-born figures on his potter's wheel (Amenhotep and his *ka*); Thoth announcing to Mutemuya, mother of Amenhotep III, that she has conceived; Mutemuya, pregnant, being taken before Isis and Khnum; Mutemuya on her bed, assisted by the deities of childbirth; the nursing of the infant and his presentation to Amon.

Behind the sanctuary, a room with two rows of eight columns leads to the most sacred room in the temple, known as the **Holy of Holies**, which was inaccessible to common mortals.

Here was kept the *statue of the great Amon*, into whose presence only the pharaoh and the highest priests were allowed to come for the purpose of celebrating the liturgical ceremonies.

The felucca is a typical Egyptian vessel, with a triangular or "Latin" sail. In ancient times, the sail was made of linen and was instead rectangular. The Nile was navigated by boats of all sizes, from those made of papyrus stalks or bundles of palms to the ten-meter feluccas and the enormous barges that transported heavy loads, including great obelisks some more than 30 meters in length, for long distances.

David Roberts loved to sketch scenes of daily life along the Nile, where boats of various types and sizes met and passed each other.

In the white mosque built inside the Temple of Amon is the sepulcher of the Fatamid sheik El Said Yussef Abu el-Haggag, who died in 1244 AD. Legend has it that his body was flown here by a host of angels. A festival that in many respects recalls the great Opet is celebrated each year in his honor.

The Egyptian columns, all with a base and an abacus, are the transposition in stone of the plants typical of the Nile valley. Originally, all the columns were painted in bright colors.

The exterior of the Museum of Luxor, the famous statue of Amenhotep II, and the exhibit of the statues brought to light in 1989 in the Temple of Amon-Ra.

THE LUXOR MUSEUM

The organization of this extremely rational museum, inaugurated in 1975 on the Nile Corniche, reflects the most modern of museographical criteria. The works on display here, only a few but all extremely important, mostly date back to the XVIII Dynasty and come from excavations in the area of Thebes, of whose historical and artistic grandeur they provide eloquent testimony.

A statue of Amenhotep II from Qurna and a stela with the same sovereign, from Karnak, stand in the **garden**; in the **entrance** is a colossal pink granite head of Amenhotep III; in the rotunda, a partially-gilded wooden head of the goddess Mehet-neret discovered in the tomb of Tutankhamen; opposite the entrance, two scribes in granite dating to the Middle Kingdom and a pink granite head of Sesostris III.

Also on the **ground floor**: a group with Amenhotep III, a statue of Thutmose III, a bust of Amenhotep II wearing the double crown of Upper and Lower Egypt, and a stela narrating the victory of Ahmose over the Hyksos.

On the **upper floor**, in addition to sculptures of various sovereigns, are display cases containing jewels, amulets, cups, tomb furnishings, votive tablets, and papyrus scrolls. One particularly elegant canopic jar in alabaster has a cover bearing the likeness Queen Tuya, mother of Ramses II.

One of the most interesting exhibits is the **Wall of the *Talatat***, the recomposition of a wall, 18 meters long and 4 meters high, from a temple built by Akhenaton in Karnak before he moved his capital on Amarna. The 283 sandstone blocks of which it is composed were found in 1925: the temple had been destroyed and the blocks used as fill for the ninth pylon of the Temple of Amon in Karnak. The myriad of small scenes that stud the wall offer an extremely interesting panorama of daily life: work in the fields, artisans at work, the beer factory, etc. The scenes on the right-hand side are more strictly religious in character and show the pharaoh and Queen Nefertiti worshiping the sun god Aton.

The beautiful gilded wood head of a cow, representing Mehet-neret. The long, curved horns are also of wood, covered with sheets of beaten copper. The head, a little over 91 cm in height, was found wrapped in a linen cloth in the Treasury of the Tomb of Tutankhamen.

An elegant stone statue of a smiling Sesostris I.

A head of Akhenaton, part of the group of colossal statues that stood in the portico of the solar Temple of Karnak.

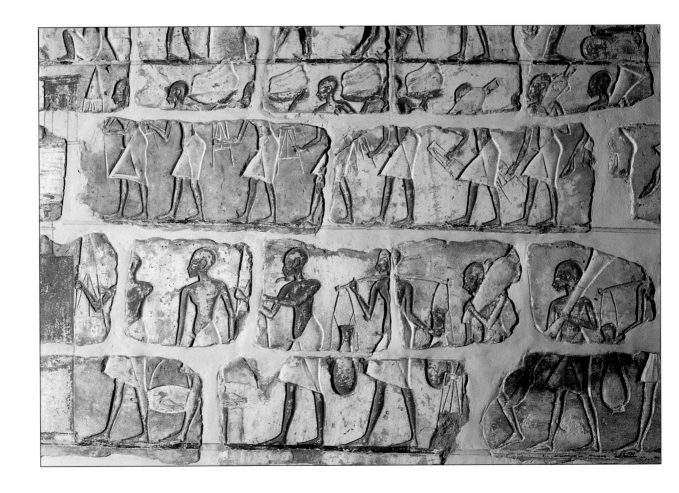

In the ninth pylon of the Temple of Karnak were found six thousand sculpted and painted talatat. Despite their having been in the main reduced to fragments, these decorations on sandstone still convey a clear picture of the great artistic revolution that accompanied the period of the Amarna heresy. Never before had scenes from daily life been depicted in a temple.

On pages 26-27, the sacred area of Karnak in a drawing by David Roberts.

The **Mummification Museum** was inaugurated in Luxor in May 1997. Such a specialized collection, which complements that of the Egyptian Museum of Cairo, with its enormous number of mummies, is a precious addition to the museum resources of the country that holds the world record as regards preservation of corpses and makes available to the public the most complete information on the subject to be found anywhere.

With a specialized library and a multimedia hall for conferences and projections for visitors, the museum exhibits the most representative archeological finds relative to the mummification techniques used in ancient Egypt, including a huge mummified crocodile, 2.25 meters in length, found in the Temple of Kom Ombo, and the mummy of Masaharta son of Pinudjem I, from the period in which this ancient science reached the height of its development (11th century BC). The exhibits are preceded by a space providing illustrations of both the process of mummification and the various phases of the 70-day journey of the dead from the moment of death to that of burial.

"Mona Lisa" in Luxor

On 22 January 1989, during investigations of the substrate in the Court of Amenhotep III in the Temple of Luxor, there came to light a group of 26 statues of gods and pharaohs. The statues were perfectly preserved, probably because they had been interred in the courtyard during the Roman occupation of the city, and their beauty and perfection places them among the masterpieces of New Kingdom sculpture. The **statue of the goddess Iunit**, from the time of Amenhotep III, is one of the most beautiful: the flawless execution exalts the charming facial expression, with its suggestion of dimples at the corners of the lips, which give the impression of a fleeting smile.

The rosy light of dawn lends perspective to the structures of the immense complex of Karnak. From left to right are distinctly visible the first pylon, Taharqa's column, and the second pylon, followed by the columns of the hypostyle hall and the obelisks of Thutmose I and of Hatshepsut. On the far right, the columns and pilasters of Thutmose III's Akh Menu and the portal of Nectanebo.

David Roberts R. A.

KARNAK

About three kilometers from the Temple of Luxor is the vast monumental area of Karnak. A mudbrick wall divides the archaeological into three separate areas: the largest is the central area, of about thirty hectares, which Diodorus Siculus tells us was the oldest and that which enclosed the dominion of **Amon**; to the south, still unexplored for about half of its extension (almost nine hectares) and linked to the first by a dromos of ram-headed sphinxes, is the dominion of the goddess **Mut**, wife of Amon and symbolically represented as a vulture; lastly, the dominion of **Munt**, the god of war, extends to the north over an area of about two and a half hectares.

On these pages, images of the avenue lined with ram-headed sphinxes that leads to the first pylon.

Facing page, top, Hector Horeau's rendition of the avenue of ram-headed sphinxes and the Euergetes Gate.

Two images of the great courtyard, built during the 22nd Dynasty, that opens behind the first pylon.
It is more than 100 meters wide; along the two sides are arrayed crouching ram-headed sphinxes, brought here from Ramses II's dromos of sphinxes. The ram was sacred to the god Amon; he protected the pharaoh, who is sculpted between the front paws of the animal.

A sphinx, with a human head, in front of the first pylon. The sphinx expedited a protective function and watched over the entrances to the temples. It was a mythical beast with the body of a crouching lion and either a human or a ram's head.

Each complex changed in size over the course of time and each successive pharaoh left his mark, either by enlarging the temples proper or by adding rooms and chapels. The structures of the three sacred complexes are identical: the main temple dedicated to the god stands at the center of each enclosure alongside the sacred lake, generally square in shape and used for ceremonies. Although all three complexes are impressive, the size of the one dedicated to Amon is astonishing.

Two images of the Temple of Seti I, located at the northwestern corner of the great courtyard. Its three chapels were consecrated to Amon, Mut, and Khonsu, and it was here that the sacred barks were stored.

THE TEMPLE OF AMON IN KARNAK

This is the largest columned temple in the world, and so architecturally complex as to provide a valid basis for study of the evolution of style from the 18th Dynasty to the end of the Ramesside era. A short **avenue of sphinxes** leads to the first pylon (the largest - 113 meters wide and 15 meters deep), the unadorned yet monumental entrance to the temple, dating to the Ptolemaic dynasty. The ram-headed sphinxes - the ram was sacred to Amon - represent the god protecting the pharaoh.

The **first courtyard**, called the Ethiopian Court, dates to the 22nd Dynasty. It is closed to the north by a portico of robust columns with closed papyrus capitals. At the feet of the columns are aligned the sphinxes Ramses II had made to flank the access to the hypostyle hall. At its center is a tall column with an open papyrus capital; it is all that remains of the gigantic, 21-meter-high, wooden-ceilinged **Pavilion of the Ethiopian King Taharqa**, which was built to shelter the sacred barks. In front and to the right of the column is the entrance to the **Temple of Ramses III**, with on three sides Osiris columns showing the pharaoh in his Jubilee garments.

KARNAK - TEMPLE OF AMON-RA

1-Sacred Lake
Begun by Thutmose III and completed by Taharqa, the sacred lake symbolized the chaotic waters of Nun, the primeval ocean that existed before the start of Creation.

2-Seventh Pylon of Thutmose III
The seventh pylon was built south of Hatshepsut's constructions and delimits the so-called "Court of the Cachette," in which more than 800 stone statues and 17,000 bronze statuettes were found in 1901.

3-Obelisk of Thutmose III
Although Thutmose III had all of 5 obelisks erected at Karnak, only two have come down to us, and neither is in Egypt: one stands in Rome's Piazza del Laterano and the other in Istanbul.

4-Peripteral Chapel
The peripteral chapel, built up against the seventh pylon, contains an alabaster sanctuary and scenes of the pharaoh Ramses II making offerings to the gods.

5-Hypostyle Hall
The hypostyle hall is found between the second pylon and the third, which forms the far wall of the space. In the complex scheme of Egyptian symbolism, the forest of stone columns may have represented the vegetation growing in the primordial marsh around the mound of creation.

6-Third Pylon of Amenhotep III
The third pylon stands at the point of intersection of the

two directional axes of the Temple of Karnak: the north-south (or terrestrial) axis, parallel to the course of the Nile, and the east-west, or celestial, axis.

7-Obelisk of Thutmose I
Four obelisks, of which only that of Thutmose I remains, stood in front of the fourth pylon at the crossing of the two axes of the Temple complex.

8-Fourth Pylon of Thutmose I
The fourth pylon, which in the time of Thutmose I was the entrance to the nucleus of the Temple of Amon, is preceded by a transverse vestibule that was dubbed "The Verdant Hall."

9-Obelisks of Hatshepsut
Of the two obelisks raised by Queen Hatshepsut only one remains. Thanks to the elegance and exquisite detail of its inscriptions, it is considered Egypt's finest.

10-Fifth Pylon of Thutmose I
The area between the fifth and sixth pylons was largely restructured by Thutmose III, who had the earlier decorations transformed to serve his own purposes.

11-Sixth Pylon of Thutmose III
The sixth is the smallest but at the same time one of the most interesting of all the pylons of Karnak. Its faces are decorated on the one side with the "Annals of Thutmose III," recording the pharaoh's victorious military campaigns, and on the other with the so-called "geographical lists" of the subject peoples of the Egyptian empire.

RECONSTRUCTION OF THE TEMPLE OF AMON-RA IN KARNAK (AXONOMETRIC PROJECTION)

1-Landing.
2-Dromos of ram-headed sphinxes (Ramses II).
3-First and largest pylon.
4-Small Temple of Seti II, with three chapels consecrated to Amon, Mut, and Khonsu.
5-Colonnade with closed-papyrus columns.
6-Pavilion of Taharqa, built to shelter the processional barks.
7-The colossus of Pinudjem.
8-Pink granite statue of Ramses II.
9-Columned doorway known as the "Portico of Bubastis."
10-Vestibule with scenes of Horemheb and Seti I making offerings to the gods.
11-Second pylon.
12-Temple of Ramses III.
13-The Great Hypostyle Hall.
14-Third pylon with the vestibule of Amenhotep III, later completed by Imhotep.
15-Exterior wall decorated with scenes of the Battle of Kadesh.
16-Courtyard of Amenhotep III.
17-Thutmose III's pink granite obelisks.
18-Thutmose I's pink granite obelisks.
19-Fourth pylon of Thutmose I.
20-Vestibule of the temple with Hatshepsut's pink granite obelisks.
21-Fifth pylon of Thutmose I.
22-Sixth pylon of Thutmose III.
23-Vestibule of the sanctuary.

24-Sanctuary of the sacred barks, in pink granite.
25-Middle Kingdom sanctuary.
26-The Akh-Menu of Thutmose III.
27-Rooms consecrated to Sokar.
28-The "Botanical Garden."
29-Small Temple of the Akh-Menu with six Osiris pillars. Two obelisks raised by Hatshepsut once stood here.
30-Sacred lake.
31-The "Lake House" of Taharqa.
32-Gate of Ramses IX.
33-Seventh pylon of Thutmose III.
34-Peripteral chapel.
35-Eighth pylon of Thutmose II and Hatshepsut.
36-Ninth pylon of Horemheb.

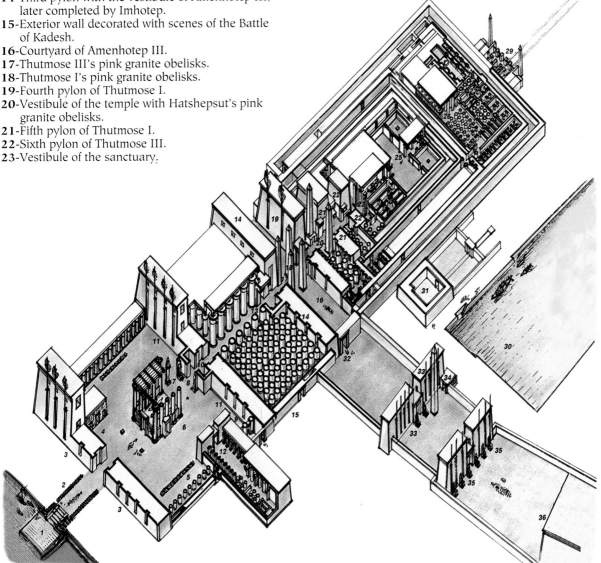

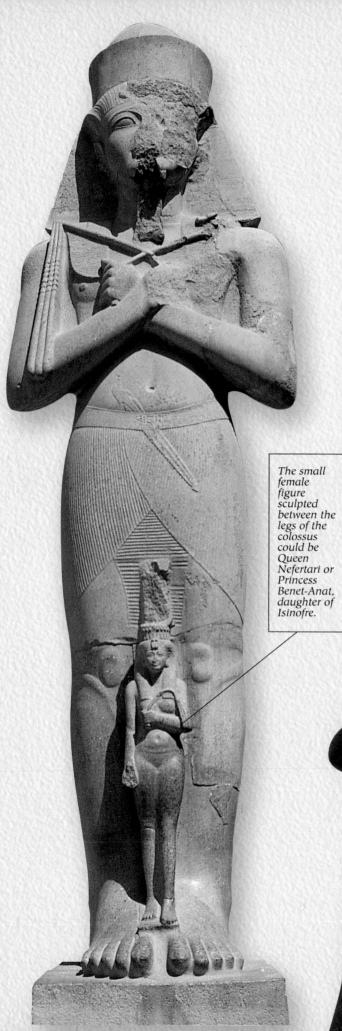

The small female figure sculpted between the legs of the colossus could be Queen Nefertari or Princess Benet-Anat, daughter of Isinofre.

Up against the second pylon is the colossal statue erected by Ramses II but usurped by Pinudjem, High Priest of Amon and pharaoh of the 21st Dynasty.

In the first courtyard is the porticoed pavilion of Taharqa, the Ethiopian king of the 25th Dynasty. It originally counted ten enormous columns; the single column remaining by the 19th century was painted by David Roberts.

On pages 36 to 39, the Temple of
Ramses III. This temple, to the right
of the Great Courtyard, may be
considered a typical example of the
architecture of the Ramesside era:
the pylon, flanked by statues of the
king, leads into a porticoed
courtyard with Osiris pillars. The
vestibule, at the far end of the court,
opens into the hypostyle atrium with
its three chapels dedicated to Amon,
Mut, and Khonsu.

Below, details of the architecture of
the temple, by Hector Horeau.

Karnac, Nov. 29th 1838

David Roberts R.A.

On the preceding pages 40 and 41, the hypostyle hall of the Temple of Amon at Karnak, as it appears today and as it was illustrated by David Roberts, who observed that the blocks scattered all over the ground were so huge as to make it difficult to imagine how they were overturned, let alone how they were ever raised.

On these pages, details of the hypostyle hall, Ramses II's architectural masterpiece. The pharaoh's coronation name "User-ma'at-ra Setep-en-ra" is carved in hieroglyphics on the barrel of one of the columns.

Set against the second pylon is a mutilated, **colossal granite statue** of Ramses II and another, 15 meters high, representing King Pinudjem. The portal, 29.5 meters high, leads into what is considered one of the most beautiful examples of Egyptian art: the **hypostyle hall**, 102 meters wide and 53 meters long, where - in a perennial challenge to the centuries - an incredible 134 columns, each 23 meters high, rise up into the sky. The tops of the open papyrus capitals were about 15 meters in circumference: standing room for fifty people.

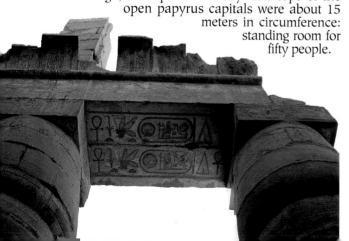

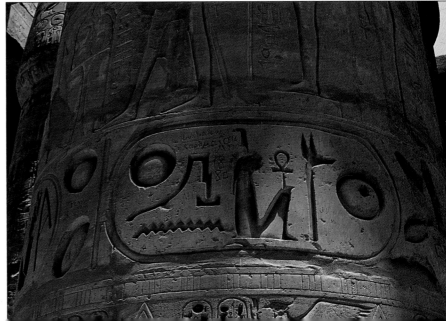

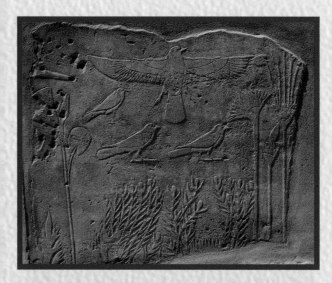

On the preceding page, top, the columns of the hypostyle hall seen from the courtyard of Amenhotep III; bottom, the architraved pillars of Thutmose III's Great Festival Hall.

On this page. Two reliefs from the so-called Botanical Garden of Thutmose III, where the pharaoh, upon his return from his expeditions in Syria, installed representations of the exotic plants and animals typical of that land.

A beautiful fasciculate papyrus column in the small courtyard near the sixth pylon.

One of pillars of Thutmose III with the papyrus, symbol of Upper Egypt.

The hall is a veritable forest of columns, and it is practically impossible to describe the emotions aroused by their size and the play of light and shadows they create. The nave, begun around 1375 BC by Amenhotep III, who conceived of the space as a simple colonnade leading to the sanctuary of Amon, is higher than the side aisles which were begun by Horemheb, continued by Seti I and Ramses II, and finally finished under Ramses IV. This difference in height made it possible to set in the wide openwork stone windows, known as *claustra*, which magically illuminated the interior. Beyond the hypostyle hall there once stood the **obelisks of Thutmose I**, each 23 meters tall and weighing 143 tons, of which only one now remains. **Hatshepsut**'s obelisk is still higher (30 meters tall and weighing 200 tons) and for its construction it is said that the queen paid no heed to cost: according to the chronicles of the time, she paid as many "bushels of gold as bags of grain." Beyond the fifth and sixth pylons (respectively of Thutmose I and Thutmose III), is the unique **Akh-Menu** of Thutmose III, the Great Festival Hall also known as the "Temple of Millions of Years." It is a fine hypostyle hall with two rows of ten columns, their shafts painted dark red in imitation of wood, and a row of thirty-two square pillars decorated with various scenes. Scarce traces of painting have come to light on some of the pillars; they are datable to the 6th century AD and tell us that this room was transformed into a church by Christian monks.

The **sacred lake** of Amon's dominion covered an area of 120
by 77 meters and was sur-
rounded by various buildings:
the storerooms, the priests'
dwellings, even an aviary for
aquatic birds. In these waters,
the priests purified themselves
every morning before beginning
the daily sacred rites.

*A view of the sacred lake and, below,
the gigantic granite scarab beetle that
Amenhotep III had sculpted in honor
of Atum Khepri. Scenes of offerings to
the sun god are engraved on the base.*

*Bottom right, the sacred area of
Karnak as seen by David Roberts.*

The Euergetes Gate (south of the Temple of Khonsu) built during the Ptolemaic period and close-packed with bas-reliefs of the pharaoh making offerings to the gods, is one of the entrances to the dominion of Amon that opened in the encircling walls.

The Temple of the Opet, built by Ptolemy VIII Euergetes II.
Detail with reliefs of a procession of gods.

The statue of the lioness-goddess Sekhmet, bride of Ptah,
stands in the right chapel. The goddess wears the solar
disk and the uraeus on her head. Sekhmet incarnates the
destructive power of the sun; she was the goddess of war
but also the deity charged with healing fractures.

The propylaea, with their columns with composite capitals, of
the Temple of Ptah, which stands against the north wall of the
dominion of Amon. Thutmose III rebuilt an earlier Middle
Kingdom mudbrick temple in limestone; Thutmose's temple
was later restored and enlarged by Shabaqa (25th dynasty)
and again by other kings of the Ptolemaic period.

The cubicle of Sesostris I, also called the White Chapel, the oldest building in the Karnak area. Considered one of the masterpieces of Middle Kingdom architecture, it was rebuilt in 1937 by Herbert Chevrier with the 77 blocks of white Tura limestone recovered from within the third pylon.

Amenhotep II's second chapel-depository in alabaster, which originally boasted wooden doors decorated with copper and gold.

Red Chapel, a gilded relief showing offerings of wine.

The Open Air Museum of Karnak. In the foreground, a pillar decorated with the image of a pharaoh offering incense.

A long line of statues of the goddess Sekhmet in Karnak's Open Air Museum.

The Open Air Museum of Karnak. The door of the Temple of Munt, built by Sesostris III.

VALLEY OF THE KINGS

The Numbering of the Tombs

It is to John Gardner Wilkinson, one of the founders of Egyptology, that we owe the numbering of the tombs in the Valley of the Kings and the chronological cataloging of the pharaohs who are buried there.

In 1927, Wilkinson set out to number the tombs according to a simple but highly efficacious system: armed with a bucket of paint and a brush, he assigned a progressive number to each tomb by painting it on the entrance or on nearby rock. He began numbering with the tomb lowest down in the Valley (that of Ramses VII, No. 1) and proceeded along the main path, numbering as he went on both the left and the right. By the time he reached the top of the Valley he had numbered 15 tombs.

He then descended again to count those in the adjacent ravines. The known and numbered tombs are today 62, all bearing the abbreviation KV for King's Valley. But a great deal of the Valley has yet to be excavated.

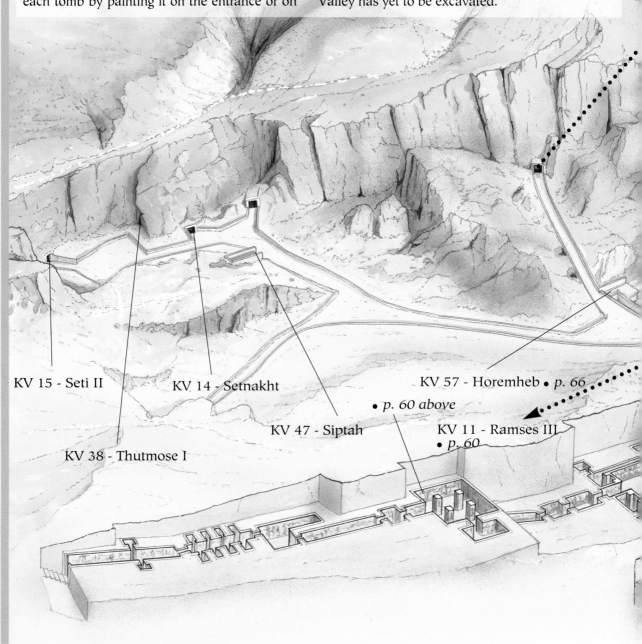

KV 15 - Seti II

KV 14 - Setnakht

KV 57 - Horemheb • *p. 66*

• *p. 60 above*

KV 47 - Siptah

KV 11 - Ramses III
• *p. 60*

KV 38 - Thutmose I

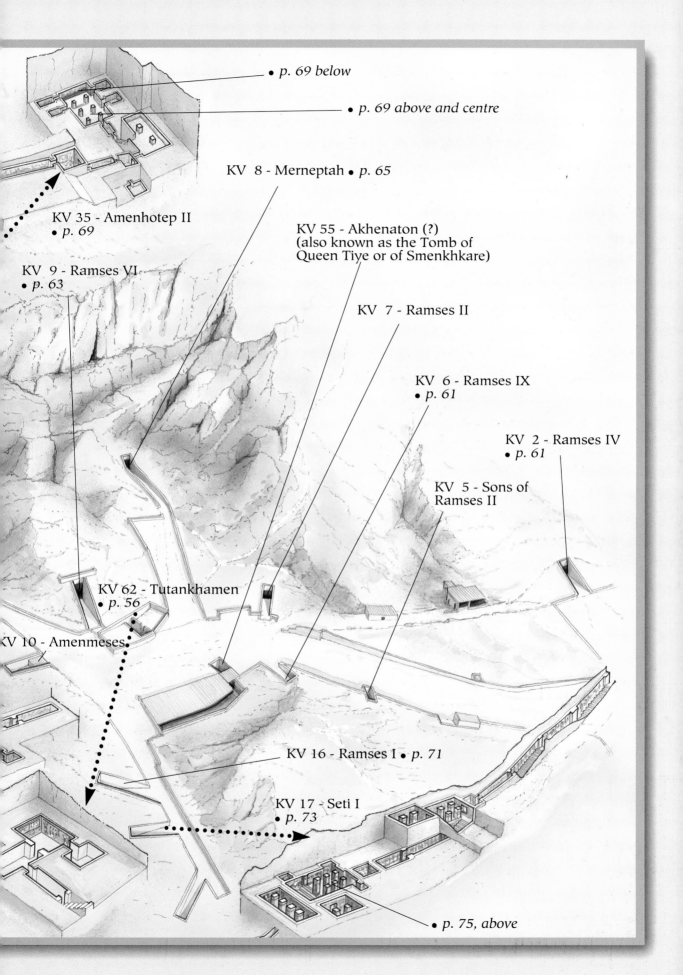

El-Qurn ("the Horn"), the pyramidal mountain that dominates the Valley of the Kings. It was consecrated to the cobra goddess Meretseger, whose name means "Beloved of the Silent One" - that is, of Osiris, the lord of the dead.

THE VALLEY OF THE KINGS

The valley of Biban el-Muluk, the **Gate of the Kings**: in this celebrated ravine, dominated by a pyramid-shaped mountain often called the "Crown of Thebes," is the necropolis of the great Egyptian sovereigns of the 18th to the 20th Dynasty.

The story of the Valley of the Kings begins with the sudden and unexpected decision of Thutmose I to separate his tomb from his mortuary temple - and moreover to bury his body not in a showy monument but in a secret, inaccessible place. His resolution brusquely interrupted a tradition that had lasted all of 1700 years! His chief architect, Ineni, excavated a shaft tomb in a lonely ravine, cut a steep stairway into the rock, and at its bottom built the sepulcher; this plan was followed by all the later pharaohs.

Ineni himself has provided us with documentation of the utmost secrecy of the undertaking, in a phrase he had carved into the wall of the mortuary chapel: "I alone oversaw the construction of the rupestral tomb of His Majesty. No one saw anything; no one heard." Actually this last phrase is not particularly credible: it is much more likely that the workers may have been prisoners of war who were eliminated when the work was completed.

But the repose of Thutmose I, like that of most of the pharaohs, was of short duration. Systematic plundering of the tombs began early, despite 24-hour surveillance by teams of guards during the entire Pharaonic period. The thieves were of course after the precious tomb furnishings; one of the objects they most coveted was the so-called "heart scarab," the amulet placed on the mummy over the heart to permit the deceased to save himself on the day of judgement, when his actions were weighed.

By a curious twist of fate, these powerful kings were destined not to find peace even after death. During the weak reign of the Ramessides, the priests of Amon, once so powerful, lost all their authority. They nevertheless remained devoted to their deceased kings, and in order to ensure them an undisturbed afterlife and to avoid profanation of the tombs, began surreptitiously transporting the royal mummies from one burial site to another. These transferrals were so frequent that Ramses III was buried all of three times! Finally, they decided to prepare a practically inaccessible secret hiding place: in the mountain of Deir el-Bahari, they had a shaft dug to a depth of about twelve meters. A long corridor led off from the bottom of the shaft into a spacious room. At night and in great secret, with only a few torches to provide light, as stealthily as the tomb raiders themselves, the priests took the pharaohs from their sarcophagi in the Valley and laid them all to rest in this cave in the mountain, each with a name shield around the neck for identification.

Some had died recently, some centuries before, some had reigned for short periods and others for decades; some had once been the most powerful rulers on earth. It made no difference. Now they lay all together, in sparse order, one alongside the next. Ahmose, the founder of the 18th Dynasty, lay beside the conqueror Thutmose III; the great Ramses II close by his father Seti I. All in all, the bodies of the pharaohs which were to remain hidden in this anonymous tomb in the heart of the mountain for three thousand years numbered forty.

A young tomb robber named Ahmed Abd el-Rasul, from the village of Qurna, discovered this hiding place by pure chance one day in 1875: for six years he and his brothers succeeded in keeping the secret, and became rich from trade in the objects they gradually stole from the royal mummies. Then the secret came out and on 5 July 1881, after lengthy questioning, the young Arab led Emil Brugsch (brother of the famous Egyptologist Heinrich and at the time vice director of the Museum of Cairo) to the entrance of the shaft. It is hard to imagine what the scholar must have felt when the flickering light of the torches illuminated the mortal remains of forty sovereigns of the ancient world! A few days later, the mummies were packed and carried down into the valley, where a ship was waiting to take them to Cairo. What happened then was both strange and moving: on hearing that the pharaohs were leaving their centuries-old tomb, the peasants of the valley and their wives crowded along the banks of the Nile, and as the ship slowly passed they rendered homage to their ancient kings, the men firing guns in the air and the women keening laments and scattering dust on their heads and breasts.

Today, the Valley of the Kings is served by a good road that for most of its length follows the route that the funeral procession must have taken.

The tombs are just as fascinating as ever: the countless graffiti on the walls mark the passage of travelers and pilgrims from Greek and Roman through modern times. One of these was the Englishman Dean Stanley, who in 1856 wrote a fine report of his journeys, remarking how seeing the tombs of the Kings was in his opinion tantamount to having seen all of Egyptian religion revealed as it appeared to the powerful of Egypt in the most salient moments of their lives.

The tombs are all more or less alike; that is, with an entrance cut into the rock wall, a sloping corridor about a hundred meters long opening on niches and various rooms, the ceilings of which are supported by pillars, and the sarcophagus room at the end.

Above, the Valley of the Kings in a 1921 photograph, with in the right foreground the tomb of Tutankhamen underneath that of Ramses VI; the archaeologist Howard Carter in an oil painting by Carter's father Samuel.

Left, the Egyptian house of Howard Carter, discoverer of the tomb of Tutankhamen, now a museum for tourists.

THE TOMB OF TUTANKHAMEN (KV 62)

The layout of the tomb of Tutankhamen is very simple: a corridor, nine meters in length, leads to the **antechamber**, off which there open on the right the **burial chamber** and the **treasury**. The antechamber also gives access to the **annex**, which contained the offers and the tomb furnishings, now considered to be one of the greatest treasures of antiquity to have come down to us intact and today in the Egyptian Museum of Cairo.

The discovery of the tomb of this boy-pharaoh who reigned only nine years and died before he was eighteen, after having restored Thebes as Egypt's capital and the ancient cult of Amon as its official religion, is one of archaeology's most fascinating stories. By 1922, the art collector and traveler Lord Carnarvon had invested about 50,000 pounds of his sizeable fortune in financing archaeological digs in Egypt. The expeditions, directed by Howard Carter, another Englishman who had begun single-mindedly searching the Valley in 1917 for the tomb

A photograph taken at the moment of the discovery shows how the outer golden chest occupied almost the entire Burial Chamber.

The frescoes of the pharaoh's funeral, on the east wall.

The quartzite sarcophagus that contained the mummy of Tutankhamen, the only one still preserved in situ *in the Valley.*

of Tutankhamen, had never turned up anything of note. Lord Carnarvon thus decided that the expedition of 1922 was to be his last in Egypt. The day of the great discovery was November 4 of that year. Almost at the base of the tomb of Ramses VI a stone step came to light; it led to a second and then a third . . . all in all, sixteen, that stopped before a plastered and sealed doorway. It appeared that even this tomb had been violated by thieves: but up to what point? And above all: would the mummy be found intact? Carter was to live the 26th of November as the "day of days:" after clearing his way to a second door on which the seals of the boy-pharaoh were intact, the archaeologist made a small hole in it. An iron bar introduced into the hole encountered only a void beyond.

Carter then tested the air with a candle and found no foul gases. Finally he put his head through the hole, and as his eyes gradually became used to the darkness, the flickering light of his candle revealed "...strange animals, statues and gold, everywhere the glitter of gold . . ."

The burial chamber contained the **sarcophagus**, a single enormous block of quartzite enclosed in four chests of gilded wood that fit one into the next. Inside the sarcophagus was the first inner sarcophagus, in wood covered with a sheet of gold inlaid with glass and semiprecious stones, showing the pharaoh as Osiris; inside this, under linen cloths and garlands of flowers, was the second inner sarcophagus, again covered with gold sheet and decorated with glass paste inlay work and semiprecious stones. No one expected, upon lifting its cover, to find a third sarcophagus - but that was exactly what it contained: a solid gold sarcophagus weighing 110.4 kg, of inestimable value for the metal alone. The king is figured wearing the headdress with the cobra and the vulture, a metal false beard, and a heavy necklace of gold and maiolica beads; in his hands he holds the flagellum and the scepter. And finally, the mummy of Tutankhamen, intact and covered with jewels and gold. The features of the king are sculpted in the extremely elegant **gold funeral mask**, inlaid with lapis lazuli, turquoise, and carnelian, that with a heavy blue-and-gold striped *nemes* with the royal symbols on the forehead covered the head and shoulders.

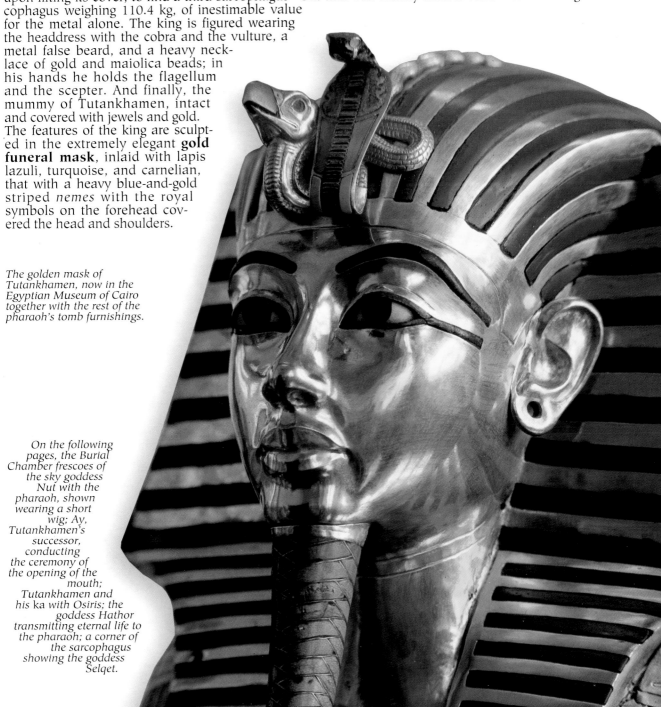

The golden mask of Tutankhamen, now in the Egyptian Museum of Cairo together with the rest of the pharaoh's tomb furnishings.

On the following pages, the Burial Chamber frescoes of the sky goddess Nut with the pharaoh, shown wearing a short wig; Ay, Tutankhamen's successor, conducting the ceremony of the opening of the mouth; Tutankhamen and his ka with Osiris; the goddess Hathor transmitting eternal life to the pharaoh; a corner of the sarcophagus showing the goddess Selqet.

Tomb of Ramses III. Portrayals of two Syrians and the pharaoh Ramses III making an offering. The Syrians are both shown with pointed beards and wearing a ribbon in their hair.

THE TOMB OF RAMSES III (KV 11)

Ramses III was the second sovereign of the 20th Dynasty and was also the last great pharaoh of the Middle Kingdom. After him came a confusing period of internecine wars and disorders, and Egypt precipitated into chaos. Ramses III initiated important administrative and social reforms. In the eighth year of his reign, he inflicted a heavy defeat on a coalition of the so-called Sea Peoples and Libyan tribes; the great battle on the Delta is illustrated in the reliefs on the walls of the Temple of Medinet Habu, where Peleset prisoners, who later settled in Palestine and called themselves Philistines, are shown along with the other Sea Peoples. In the 29th year of his reign, Ramses III fell victim to a palace conspiracy, as we learn from a scroll known as the *Judicial Papyrus*, now in the Egyptian Museum of Turin, that documents the capture and judging of the guilty parties. The tomb is also known as "Bruce's Tomb," from the name of its discoverer, and as the "Harper's Tomb," from the frescoes which show several men playing the harp in honor of the gods - a quite unusual subject in Egyptian art. The pharaoh's sarcophagus, a splendid block of pink granite, was removed from the tomb by the Paduan archaeologist Giovanni Battista Belzoni and later sold to the king of France, who exhibited it in the Louvre.

THE TOMB OF RAMSES IV (KV 2)

The first tomb along the approach to the center of the Valley is small (66 meters long), but contains the sarcophagus of Ramses IV, sovereign of the 20th Dynasty and son of Ramses III. As early as the 5th century, it was used as a church by a small Christian community in the Valley. The plan of the tomb appears on a papyrus in the Egyptian Museum of Turin. The splendid decorations of the tomb are predominately texts, with scenes from the *Book of the Dead* (*Am-Tuat*), the *Book of the Gates*, and the *Book of the Caverns*.

THE TOMB OF RAMSES IX (KV 6)

This unfortunately quite damaged tomb belongs to one of the last Ramessides of the 20th Dynasty, whose reigns were

Tomb of Ramses IV. The corridor leading to the chamber containing the sarcophagus. It is one of the largest found in the Valley, measuring 3.30 meters in length by 2.74 in height. The cover is adorned with a relief of the pharaoh between the goddesses Isis and Nephthys.

Tomb of Ramses IX. The pharaoh is shown twice, once with the white crown of Upper Egypt and again with the red crown of Lower Egypt.

marked by a long series of domestic disorders and by famines.

When it was opened, the tomb was found to contain an enormous pair of skids from the sledge on which the pharaoh's bark was transported. Another interesting find consisted of several hundred shards on which the tomb laborers had recorded the number of tools, the hours of work, the list of provisions, etc.

The tomb consists of a long staircase leading to a corridor that opens onto two rooms, one of which with four pillars, and a second smaller corridor that ends at the sarcophagus chamber.

Tomb of Ramses IX. Top, symbolic scenes with the sacred scarab and the sun, Ra; left, a detail of the sacred texts engraved in hieroglyphics on one wall of the corridor; bottom left, two protector goddesses with a serpent "who is in the earth" and a scarab; bottom right, the bark of the ram-headed sun god Ra (that is, the "sun of the night") with facing the goddess Nebetuia ("the lady of the bark") - a form of Hathor - the gods Upuaut ("he who opens the way") and Sia ("knowledge"), and the benign serpents. Scenes from the Book of the Caverns.

Facing page, tomb of Ramses VI. Two details of the decoration of the ceiling of the burial chamber, with the goddess Nut and the stellar goddesses; the decoration of a pillar, showing the ibis-headed god Thoth with the waxing moon; the burial chamber with the sarcophagus, as seen by Hector Horeau.

THE TOMB OF RAMSES VI (KV 9)

Known as the Tomb of Memnon by the Romans and also as La Tombe de la Métempsychose (Napoleonic expedition, 1798), the tomb of Ramses VI was discovered by the Englishman James Burton. Like the other great Ramesside tombs, its entrance is high, about 400 meters above the valley bottom, exactly the contrary of the deeply-sunk tombs of the 18th Dynasty.

The front part is the oldest and was begun for Ramses V. The final, enlarged plan is quite linear, with a corridor leading to an antechamber,

a pillared hall, a second corridor, and a second antechamber that precedes the burial chamber, which has an - **astronomical ceiling** entirely decorated with astronomical scenes and the creation of the sun. A gigantic sky goddess Nut, repeated twice, towers above all and enfolds the western sphere. The many Greek and Coptic graffiti on the walls indicate that the tomb, in which many remains of the workers' tools were found, was known and visited from oldest times.

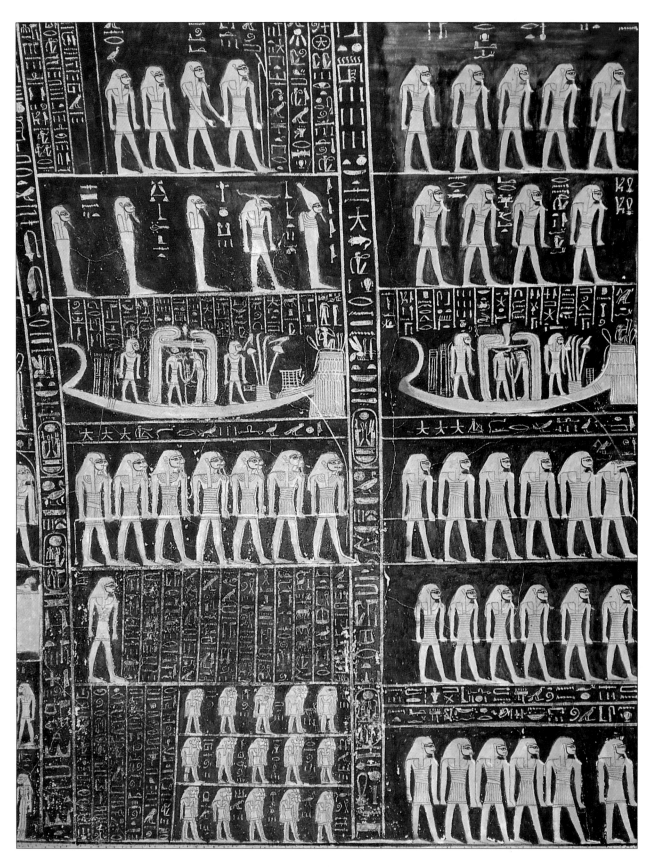

Tomb of Ramses VI. A detail of the ceiling of the burial (sarcophagus) chamber, showing the stellar gods in a great procession led by the solar barks. The scenes illustrated on the ceiling are taken from the Book of the Day *and the* Book of the Night. *The walls of the chamber are instead decorated with scenes from the* Book of the Earth.

The Tomb of Merneptah (KV 8)

Merneptah, the fourth pharaoh of the 19th Dynasty, who came to power rather late in life, was the thirteenth son of Ramses II and Isinofre.

The plan of his tomb is simple: a long, sectioned corridor that descends to a three-aisle hypostyle hall, in which the cover of the sarcophagus is preserved. The cover, in the form of a royal seal, is in red granite sculpted to the likeness of the pharaoh wearing the *nemes* headdress, with his arms crossed and holding the scepter and flagellum in his hands.

The pharaoh's mummy was not in the sarcophagus when it was discovered, and this fact gave rise to speculation that Merneptah may have been the pharaoh who chased Moses on his flight from Egypt and drowned in the Red Sea - but the mummy was found in 1898, in the tomb of Amenhotep II, where it had probably been moved for safekeeping.

In a painting in the tomb of Merneptah, the pharaoh, with on his head the atef crown with two feathers and rams' horns, stands before the falcon-headed god Horus.

A detail of the pillared room in the tomb of Merneptah.

The Stela of Victory

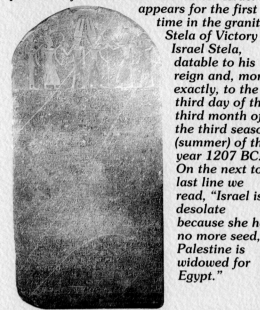

*I*f his father Ramses II is considered the pharaoh of the slavery of the Hebrews in Egypt, Merneptah is known as the pharaoh of the Exodus. The name "Israel" appears for the first time in the granite Stela of Victory or Israel Stela, datable to his reign and, more exactly, to the third day of the third month of the third season (summer) of the year 1207 BC. On the next to last line we read, "Israel is desolate because she has no more seed, Palestine is widowed for Egypt."

The pharaoh Horemheb making an offering of two globe-shaped vases.
The small pictures on the right show examples of the hieroglyphics painted on the walls of the tomb of Horemheb. From top to bottom, a hawk, a duck (a Dafila acuta or Pintail), the falcon identifying Horus (phonetic value = hr), and a resting cobra (phonetic value = ḏt) over a reed.

On the facing page, the cartouches with the name of the pharaoh Horemheb, "Meryamon Djeser-kheperu-ra Setep-en-ra."

THE TOMB OF HOREMHEB (KV 57)

Horemheb, the last pharaoh of the 18th Dynasty, was not of royal blood; from a family of governors, he had been chief of the archers under Amenhotep IV, of whom he was a great friend, and rose to the rank of general; he succeeded Tutankhamen and Ay on the throne, destroyed all symbols of the heretic Atonian religion and surcharged his immediate predecessors' cartouches with his own. Among his most brilliant undertakings was the peace stipulated with the Hittite king Mursilis II.

The English archaeologist Edward Ayrton found the name of the general-pharaoh, in hieratic script, on a tablet regarding inspections of the royal tombs in the Valley, and thus succeeded in locating the tomb, which represents a transition from the simple, bent-axis tombs of the

18th Dynasty to the more elaborate ones that were to come; the corridor, after a slight initial deviation, proceeds in a practically straight line to the burial chamber. The eyes of the archaeologists who discovered the tomb were greeted by **bas-reliefs**, which while depicting the usual funeral repertory were brilliantly colored and as perfect, fresh, and luminous as if they had just been painted.

Examples of the splendid mural decoration of the tomb of Horemheb, with the principal deities of the Egyptian pantheon. Isis, shown with the hieroglyph of her name on her head; Hathor with bovine horns and the solar disk; Amentit, the funerary goddess of the west; Ptah, the god of the underworld, shown in mummy form wearing the skullcap; Horus, with the head of a falcon and the double crown of Upper and Lower Egypt.

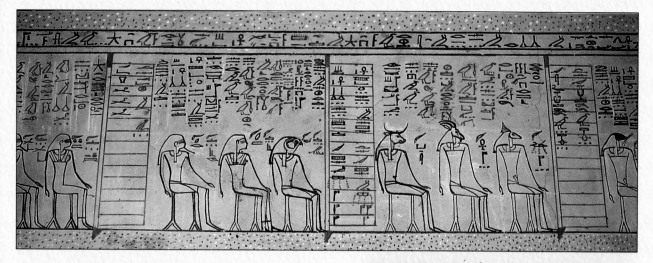

Above, a detail of the decoration of the tomb; center, a pillar in the vestibule showing the pharaoh receiving the ankh from the goddess Hathor; bottom, the quartzite sarcophagus in which the king's mummy was found.

THE TOMB OF AMENHOTEP II (KV 35)

This tomb, discovered by Victor Loret in 1898, is one of the most interesting in the Valley in terms of both architecture and decoration.

The burial chamber contains the great **quartzite sarcophagus**, which when it was discovered still contained the pharaoh's mummy, with a garland of mimosa flowers encircling the neck. In an annex off the burial chamber, Loret found nine more sarcophagi, containing the mummies of the pharaohs Amenhotep III, Thutmose IV, Merneptah, Siptah, Seti II, Setnakht, Ramses IV, Ramses V, and Ramses VI.

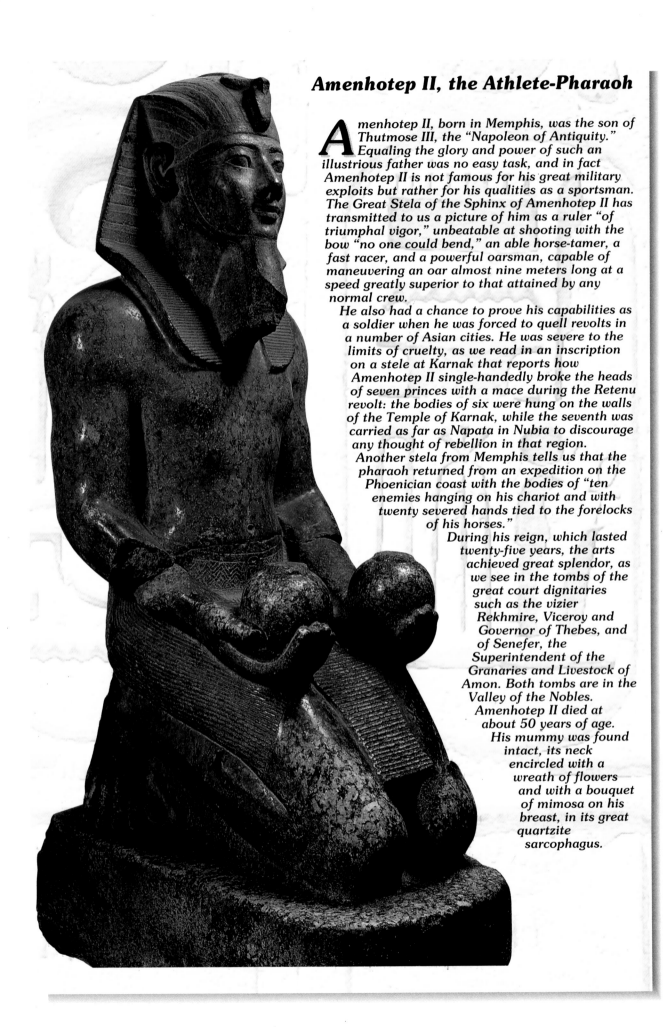

Amenhotep II, the Athlete-Pharaoh

Amenhotep II, born in Memphis, was the son of Thutmose III, the "Napoleon of Antiquity." Equaling the glory and power of such an illustrious father was no easy task, and in fact Amenhotep II is not famous for his great military exploits but rather for his qualities as a sportsman. The Great Stela of the Sphinx of Amenhotep II has transmitted to us a picture of him as a ruler "of triumphal vigor," unbeatable at shooting with the bow "no one could bend," an able horse-tamer, a fast racer, and a powerful oarsman, capable of maneuvering an oar almost nine meters long at a speed greatly superior to that attained by any normal crew.

He also had a chance to prove his capabilities as a soldier when he was forced to quell revolts in a number of Asian cities. He was severe to the limits of cruelty, as we read in an inscription on a stele at Karnak that reports how Amenhotep II single-handedly broke the heads of seven princes with a mace during the Retenu revolt: the bodies of six were hung on the walls of the Temple of Karnak, while the seventh was carried as far as Napata in Nubia to discourage any thought of rebellion in that region.

Another stela from Memphis tells us that the pharaoh returned from an expedition on the Phoenician coast with the bodies of "ten enemies hanging on his chariot and with twenty severed hands tied to the forelocks of his horses."

During his reign, which lasted twenty-five years, the arts achieved great splendor, as we see in the tombs of the great court dignitaries such as the vizier Rekhmire, Viceroy and Governor of Thebes, and of Senefer, the Superintendent of the Granaries and Livestock of Amon. Both tombs are in the Valley of the Nobles.

Amenhotep II died at about 50 years of age. His mummy was found intact, its neck encircled with a wreath of flowers and with a bouquet of mimosa on his breast, in its great quartzite sarcophagus.

Below, the serpent Apophis, symbol of evil, in perennial conflict with the light of the sun god Ra.

Ramses I between Horus (left) and Anubis (right). The pharaoh's cartouches carry the last two parts of his coronation name: Ramses Men-pehty-ra ("Ra has fashioned him; Eternal is the Strength of Ra").

THE TOMB OF RAMSES I (KV 16)

The founder of the 19th Dynasty was a regular army officer, a general, and the vizier of Horemheb. His reign was very brief, barely two years, but in this period - as witnessed by the bas-reliefs in the hypostyle hall of Karnak - he advanced into Hittite territory "as far as the land of Kadesh." He immediately took his son Seti I as co-regent and chose Tanis as capital of the empire.

The structure of his tomb, discovered by Belzoni, is rather spare, since evidently the elderly pharaoh died suddenly while work was still in progress.

THE TOMB OF SETI I (KV 17)

The tomb of Seti I is one of the most spectacular in the Valley of the Kings, and the pharaoh who was buried there was also one of the most important of his dynasty, the 19th. Son of Ramses I, he was chief archer and vizier while his father lived. As pharaoh, Seti I continued the policy of expansion into the East: he advanced into Syria as far as Tyre, drove back the advance of the Hittite chief Muwatallis, and recaptured Phoenicia.

The tomb, discovered in October of 1817 by Belzoni and known at length by the archaeologist's name alone, is 105 meters long; 27 steep steps descend immediately to a much lower level. Here, a corridor leads to a second flight of steps leading to a second corridor ending in a room in which Belzoni found a shaft, evidently dug to confuse unwanted visitors.

Facing page, top, the Third Division of the Book of the Gates; bottom, two walls of the tomb of Ramses I. One shows the solar bark with Ra and the struggle between Amon and Apophis, while the adjacent wall depicts Ramses I offering two vases to the god Nefertum.

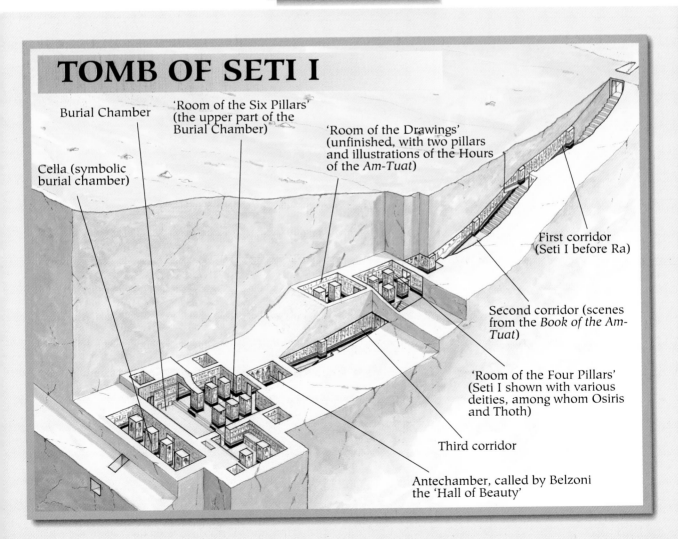

TOMB OF SETI I

Burial Chamber

'Room of the Six Pillars' (the upper part of the Burial Chamber)

'Room of the Drawings' (unfinished, with two pillars and illustrations of the Hours of the *Am-Tuat*)

Cella (symbolic burial chamber)

First corridor (Seti I before Ra)

Second corridor (scenes from the *Book of the Am-Tuat*)

'Room of the Four Pillars' (Seti I shown with various deities, among whom Osiris and Thoth)

Third corridor

Antechamber, called by Belzoni the 'Hall of Beauty'

Tomb of Seti I. Right, a detail of the pharaoh in a bas-relief on a pillar in the first room; above, Osiris between two fetishes; below, a scene from the Book of the Am-Tuat with the solar bark of Ra, shown with the head of a ram.

Belzoni noted a crack of 65 centimeters on the opposite wall; after daringly crossing the shaft, he widened the opening and discovered that it led to rooms the original builders had hoped to keep hidden. Even so, none of these contained the sarcophagus: as it turned out, Belzoni was only halfway there. More corridors, more staircases, and more rooms finally led him to the sarcophagus chamber - but not the mummy, which was discovered only seventy years later, in Deir el-Bahari, while the lovely sarcophagus is today part of the Soane Collection in London. What is so odd and unusual about this tomb is the fact that it apparently was supposed to go even deeper into the heart of the earth. Belzoni began exploring a mysterious gallery that starts under the sarcophagus, but after about ninety meters the lack of air and the friability of the rock forced him to stop; another thirty meters were excavated in the 1950s. The gallery is still a mystery, since no one knows what it was for and where it leads. But an ancient Valley legend tells of a tunnel that crosses the mountain and emerges near the temple of Hatshepsut at Deir el-Bahari . . .

Belzoni thought this was the finest tomb ever discovered in Egypt; the walls, columns, and ceilings are in fact literally covered with painted and bas-relief **decoration** full of meaning and symbolism.

Tomb of Seti I. Top, a portrayal of the gods of the underworld; center, the realm of the Tuat separated from that of Osiris by a wall with gates protected by guardians; bottom, the serpent surrounding and protecting the tabernacle on the bark bearing the ram-headed god Ra.

THE TOMB OF THUTMOSE III (KV 34)

This tomb was discovered in 1898 by Victor Loret, who had succeeded Gaston Maspero as Director of the Egyptian government Antiquities Service.

The entrance to the tomb was hidden in a crevice about ten meters above the valley bottom: two corridors with two steep flights of stairs led to a ritual well that terminated in a vestibule with two pilasters.

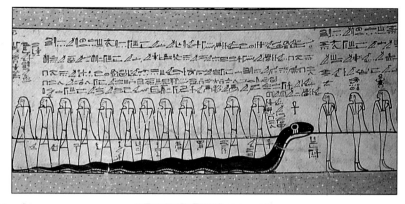

Above and facing page, the texts inscribed on the walls of the tomb, which are decorated with scenes illustrating the Book of the Am-Tuat; that is, the description of the sun god's nightly journey through the otherworld.

Thutmose III, the "Napoleon of Antiquity"

Thutmose III must have been about thirty-seven years of age at the death of his little-loved aunt and stepmother Hatshepsut, in whose shadow he had lived for all the twenty-five years during which she had reigned as sole and absolute monarch. The forced exile to which he had been subjected for so long had so humiliated him that, after having removed the most important officials from their key posts, he indulged in his own belated vendetta by erasing the name, the cartouches, and the images of Hatshepsut from almost all the monuments in Egypt. This puerile first act as new ruler, however, did nothing to obscure his innate greatness and the importance: in the long run, Thutmose III proved to be probably the greatest pharaoh Egypt ever had. It was the American archaeologist James Henry Breasted who dubbed him the "Napoleon of Antiquity." Hatshepsut had left Thutmose III a stable and pacific realm, but her prolonged policy of non-intervention had permitted a whole series of small principalities and kingdoms to grow up along the eastern borders of the country. By Thutmose III's time they were ready to join forces to oppose the prosperous and close-at-hand Egypt. Among all of these, the kingdom of the Mitanni, in northern Mesopotamia, was the most worrisome. The seventeen military campaigns conducted by Thutmose III in Syria were all marked by an outstanding strategic sense and a thorough knowledge of military tactics. The list of Thutmose's conquests, inscribed on the walls of the Temple of Amon at Karnak, includes the names of 350 cities that were overcome by his armies. The eighth campaign, conducted near the end of the thirty-third year of his reign, was to have been the decisive attack into the heart of the Mitanni kingdom. At the start, Thutmose III grouped his troops at Gaza. Then he moved on to Byblos, where he ordered the construction of many cedar-wood ships that were loaded onto heavy four-wheeled wagons drawn by oxen. Thus, after having traveled 250 kilometers overland, the pharaoh's army was able to cross the Euphrates River. The decisive battle took place west of Aleppos near the city of Karkhemesh. When Thutmose III died, one mid-March, he was about seventy years old. He left behind him a stable, rich country, an efficient public administration, and a huge empire stretching from the Euphrates to the fourth cataract of the Nile, in Sudan.

Sharply to its left was the burial chamber.

Its curious form, that of a cartouche, repeats the ovoid of the massive sarcophagus in red quartzite found at the northwest end of the room. When it was discovered, its cover lay broken on the floor - but the mummy of the pharaoh had been safely recovered seventeen years earlier in the Deir el-Bahari hideaway.

The Tomb of Thutmose III is

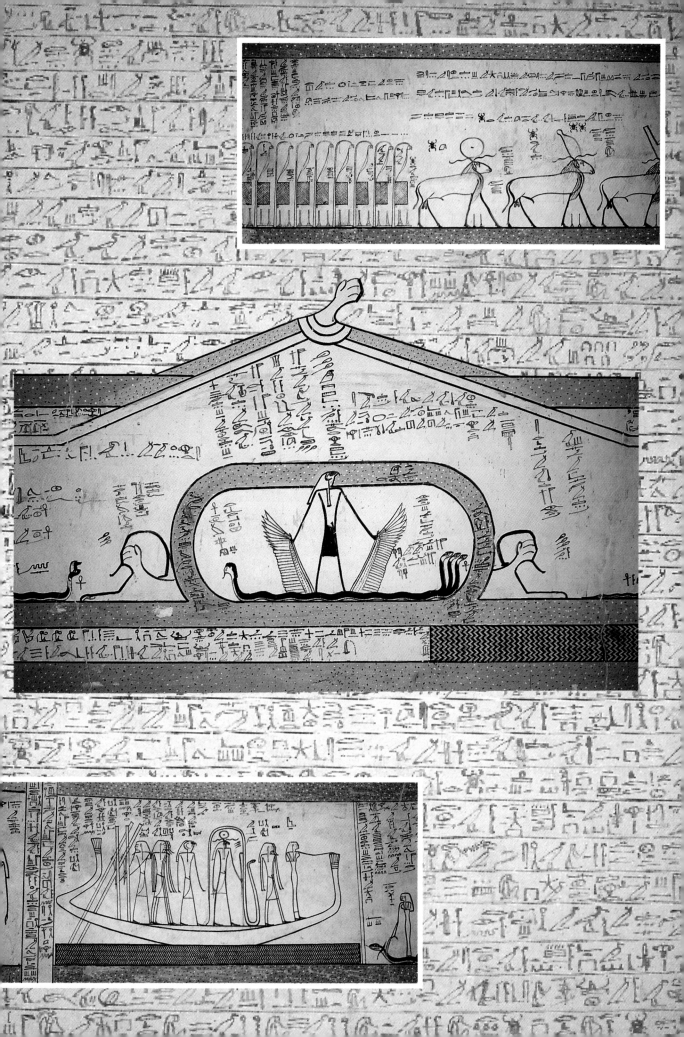

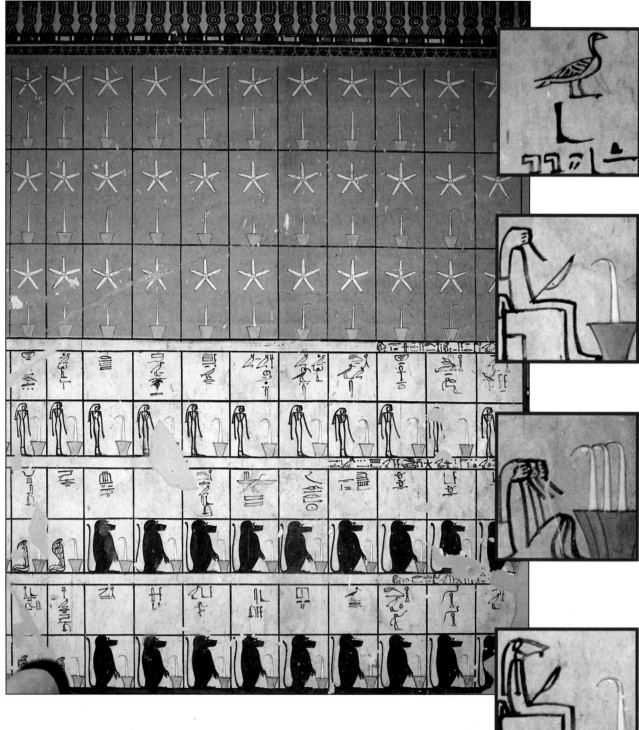

Tomb of Thutmose III. The vestibule of the tomb is decorated with schematic and symbolic representations of the offers to the stellar gods, to the attendant spirits of the otherworld, and to dog-headed deities.

unique among the Valley sepulchers.

The type of writing used here is cursive hieroglyphic, the colors are soft and rosy, and the decorations are all painted, with no bas-reliefs to be found. Loret's impression of the curved walls of the room was of "an enormous papyrus scroll." Almost all of the tomb decoration illustrates the *Book of the Dead (Am-Tuat)*; biographical reference to the pharaoh is found only in one small scene on a pilaster in the burial chamber, where he is depicted with a following of some of his wives, and in another a little further on that shows him being nursed by his mother Isis, whose breast hangs from the branch of the sycamore tree with which the goddess is identified. A New Kingdom scribe by the name of Amenophis viewed this scene and was apparently quite struck by it, since he left us his name inscribed on the wall alongside the comment, "A thousand times beautiful is the painting below."

THE VALLEY OF THE QUEENS

The Valley of the Queens, located southwest of the Valley of the Kings, also goes by the name of Biban el-Harim, but the ancient Egyptians called it Ta Set Neferu, meaning "place of the kings' sons," since it was here that, from the 23rd Dynasty onward, the royal princes and princesses were buried. The sepulchers in the Valley (about 110 have been found to date) range from simple, unadorned shaft tombs to true architectural complexes embellished with wall paintings. From 1903 through 1906, a team of Italian archaeologists worked here under the direction of Ernesto Schiaparelli, to whom we owe the discovery of many tombs, including that of Nefertari, considered to be the most beautiful at Thebes.

Khaemwese offering a large feather to the gods.

The prince Amon-her-Khopsef and the god Khnum.

TOMB OF KHAEMWESE (QV 44)

TOMB OF AMON-HER-KHOPSEF (QV 55)

Detail of the face of Nefertari.

TOMB OF QUEEN NEFERTARI (QV 66)

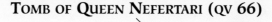

TOMB OF NEFERTARI

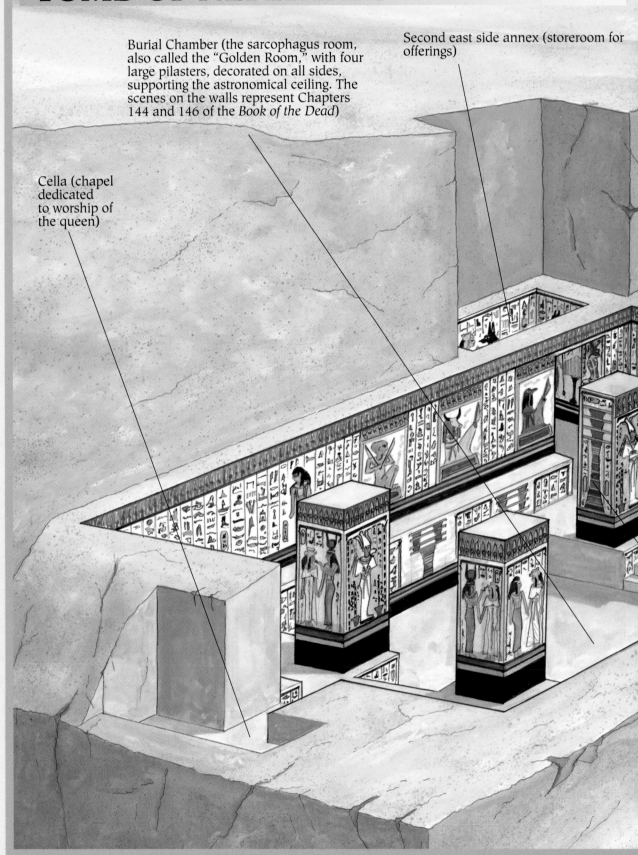

Burial Chamber (the sarcophagus room, also called the "Golden Room," with four large pilasters, decorated on all sides, supporting the astronomical ceiling. The scenes on the walls represent Chapters 144 and 146 of the *Book of the Dead*)

Second east side annex (storeroom for offerings)

Cella (chapel dedicated to worship of the queen)

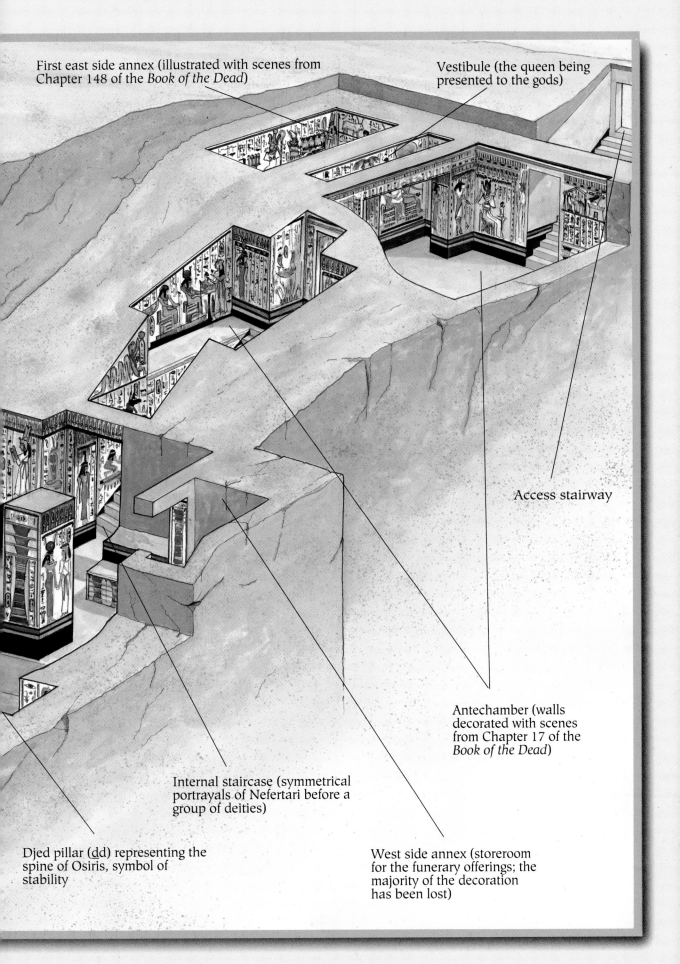

First east side annex (illustrated with scenes from Chapter 148 of the *Book of the Dead*)

Vestibule (the queen being presented to the gods)

Access stairway

Antechamber (walls decorated with scenes from Chapter 17 of the *Book of the Dead*)

Internal staircase (symmetrical portrayals of Nefertari before a group of deities)

Djed pillar (d̲d) representing the spine of Osiris, symbol of stability

West side annex (storeroom for the funerary offerings; the majority of the decoration has been lost)

THE TOMB OF NEFERTARI

This tomb, discovered in 1904 by the Italian Ernesto Schiaparelli, was dug into the west flank of the valley for Nefertari, Meri-en-Mut, wife of Ramses II and without doubt the best-loved of the many wives of this great pharaoh, who built the architectural jewel of the Small Temple of Abu Simbel for her. The tomb is 27.5 meters long and lies about eight meters below ground level: since the layer of rock into which it is dug is particularly friable, the walls were bonded with such a thick layer of plaster that their pictorial decoration seems to be in relief. When the tomb was discovered, it was immediately apparent that it had been violated from early times: all the tomb furnishings had disappeared and the mummy of the woman who had been one of the most famous queens of Egypt was nothing but miserable remains. Only the splendid **paintings** remained to bear witness to the fact that this tomb was in its time the most important and loveliest of the entire Valley of the Queens.

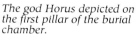

The god Horus depicted on the first pillar of the burial chamber.

The red-crowned serpent representing the goddess Nekhbet.

Nefertari, "Boundless in her Love, Beautiful of Face"

I n the harem given by the pharaoh Seti I to his son Ramses while he was still crown prince, two women surpassed all the others in beauty: Nefertari, the first wife, and Isinofre. We know nothing, with certainty, of their origins and families, although the knob of a blue-enameled coffer (now in Cairo's Egyptian Museum) bearing the cartouche of the pharaoh Ay has led scholars to suggest that Queen Nefertari might have descended from the family of that ruler and may even have been Ay's daughter or niece. The slim and elegant Nefertari was much loved by Ramses II and appeared at his side at official and religious ceremonies as the Great Royal Wife. Isinofre, also a Great Royal Wife, instead preferred to remain in the shadows. Queen Nefertari bore four sons (Amon-her-Khopsef, Pa-Re-her-Wenemef, Mery-Re, and Mery-Atum) and two daughters, Meritamon and Nebet-Tani, both of whom later became wives and queens to Ramses II.

Nefertari died between the 26th and 30th year of her husband's reign; in the Small Temple of Abu Simbel she is often attributed the status of "living," even though we know her demise predated completion of the temple (34th year); the third pilaster in the south row in the vestibule shows Benet-Anat, daughter of Isinofre, as queen.

Nefertari, Meri-en-Mut, whose names mean "the most beautiful among them" and "beloved of Mut," had many appellations, among which "boundless in her love, beautiful of face, elegant with the two feathers, dulcet in love, Mistress of the Two Lands," but above all "Ruler of all the Lands," a title normally not attributed queens and therefore evidence of the high esteem in which Queen Nefertari was held.

These depictions have provided us with much information about the complex religious world and the spiritual beliefs of the New Kingdom Egyptians.

The various attempts made between 1934 and 1977 to check the degradation of the tomb obtained no appreciable results; worse, some of the restoration techniques used even altered the colors of the paintings. In 1986, an agreement between the Egyptian Antiquities Service and the Getty Conservation Institute launched a systematic project for recovery of the tomb. An international team began studying the various problem areas, and it was discovered that rock salt, the major component of which is sodium chloride, was the agent mainly responsible for the damage to the tomb. Restoration work began in 1988. The first step was to apply Japanese paper to immobilize the fragments of detached plaster and prevent them from falling; then and only then was it possible to remove the dust (using dentist's tools), reinforce the plaster and

From top to bottom, Nefertari asking Thoth for his bowl and scribe's tablet in order to obtain the god's magical power; the god Khepri; the vulture, symbol of the goddess Nekhbet.

inject a special compound to fill the cracks, and finally smooth over the points of conjunction with fresh plaster.

After cleaning with another special product applied with cotton swabs, the colors regained their original brilliance - so perfect were they that there was found to be no need for any retouching. Work was concluded in April 1992, but for the following three years the tomb was kept under observation by experts, who finally gave their okay for reopening to the public in November 1995.

The cartouche of Queen Nefertari, Meri-en-Mut; Isis and Nephthys with the god Ra with the head of a ram. The hieroglyphic text reads, "Osiris reposes in Ra, Ra is he in whom Osiris reposes."

The burial chamber with the djed pillars; the djed is the symbol of stability.

85

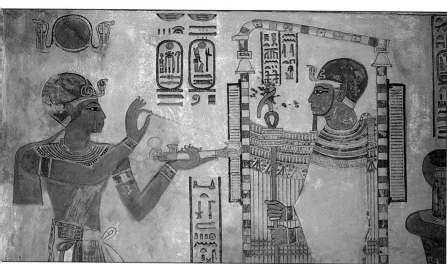

The pharaoh Ramses III embraced by the goddess Isis and Prince Amon-her-Khopsef, who is shown, like any Egyptian boy, with a shorn head and a single braid to one side; the pharaoh Ramses III facing the god of Memphis, Ptah; the pharaoh with Hapi.

THE TOMB OF AMON-HER-KHOPSEF

This tomb was originally built to contain the remains of another prince and son of Ramses III, and only later became that of Amon-her-Khopsef, son of the same father and Queen Nefertari. Extremely simple in structure - a staircase leads to a square room and a corridor, which in turn leads to the sarcophagus room - the tomb is characterized by decoration in lively, intense colors; an unusual shade of turquoise predominates throughout.

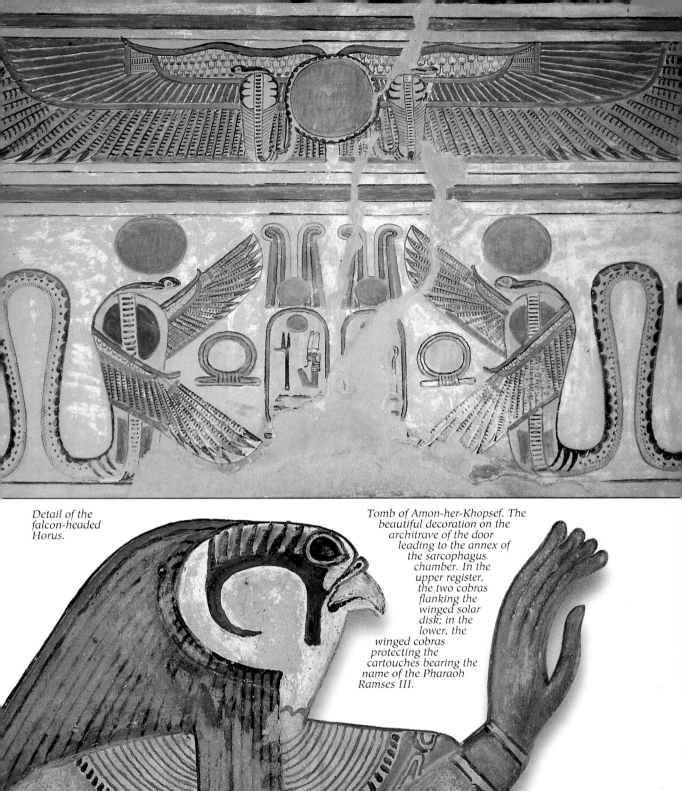

Detail of the falcon-headed Horus.

Tomb of Amon-her-Khopsef. The beautiful decoration on the architrave of the door leading to the annex of the sarcophagus chamber. In the upper register, the two cobras flanking the winged solar disk; in the lower, the winged cobras protecting the cartouches bearing the name of the Pharaoh Ramses III.

The decoration of the first room shows the pharaoh presenting his young son to various divinities: Thoth, Ptah, and the four sons of Horus (Hapi, Imset, Duamuttef and Qebesenuf). The quartet, after having participated with Anubis in the mummification rites of Osiris, became the protectors of the canopic jars.

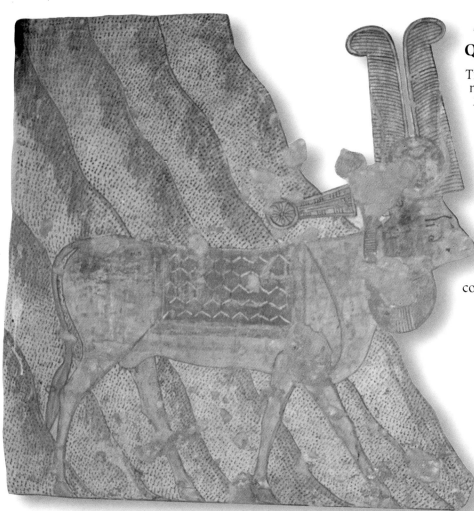

THE TOMB OF QUEEN TITI

Titi was the wife of one of the numerous Ramses' of the 20th Dynasty, perhaps Ramses IV. Her long-abandoned tomb, which has over time been put to many uses - even being made a stable for donkeys! - is in very poor condition despite attempts at preservation; it is nevertheless distinguished by its interesting limestone relief decoration dominated by a light rose color.

Tomb of Queen Titi. The goddess Hathor in bovine form, exiting from a mountain. On one of the unfortunately spoiled walls of this tomb, Giovanni Belzoni inscribed his name.

THE TOMB OF PRINCE PA-RE-HER-WENEMEF

Pa-Re-her-Wenemef was another of the sons of Ramses III, who died very young and who, like his brothers, was buried in this valley. The decoration of this tomb is quite similar to that of the others of its kind; in other words, the deceased prince is shown being presented to the various gods by his father. The predominant colors here, however, are yellow ocher and pink.

Tomb of Pa-Re-her-Wenemef.
The gates of the realm of the Tuat presided over by guardians.
Right, a guardian shown frontally and two other guardians: one, the crocodile-headed Sobek, the other vulture-headed.
Below, two crouching baboons and another, standing baboon armed with a long knife.

THE TOMB OF KHAEMWESE

Prince Khaemwese, another son of Ramses III and probably the younger brother of Amon-her-Khopsef, was given a tomb that much recalls those of the kings in its ground plan, even though, naturally, it is much smaller. It is, however, the largest of all the tombs of the sons of Ramses III, and consists of a gallery divided into two sectors on which there open a vestibule with two side annexes, the burial chamber, and a rear annex. When the tomb was discovered in 1903, the corridor was almost completely blocked by sarcophagi - and in fact it was discovered that the tomb had been "recycled" numerous times after Khaemwese's entombment. Like in the tombs of other princes, the decoration is quite lively, with scenes of offerings and tributes in intense, brilliant colors.

Tomb of Khaemwese.
The goddess Isis, sister and wife of Osiris, shown standing in human form; Serqet, the scorpion goddess, shown in human form with her symbol on her head.

*Tomb of Khaemwese.
The pharaoh Ramses
III making an offering to
the gods. The scenes
decorating the walls of the
gallery show the prince
accompanied by his father at the
ceremony of offering and
presentation to the gods. In the side
chambers the ceremony continues,
but with the prince alone.*

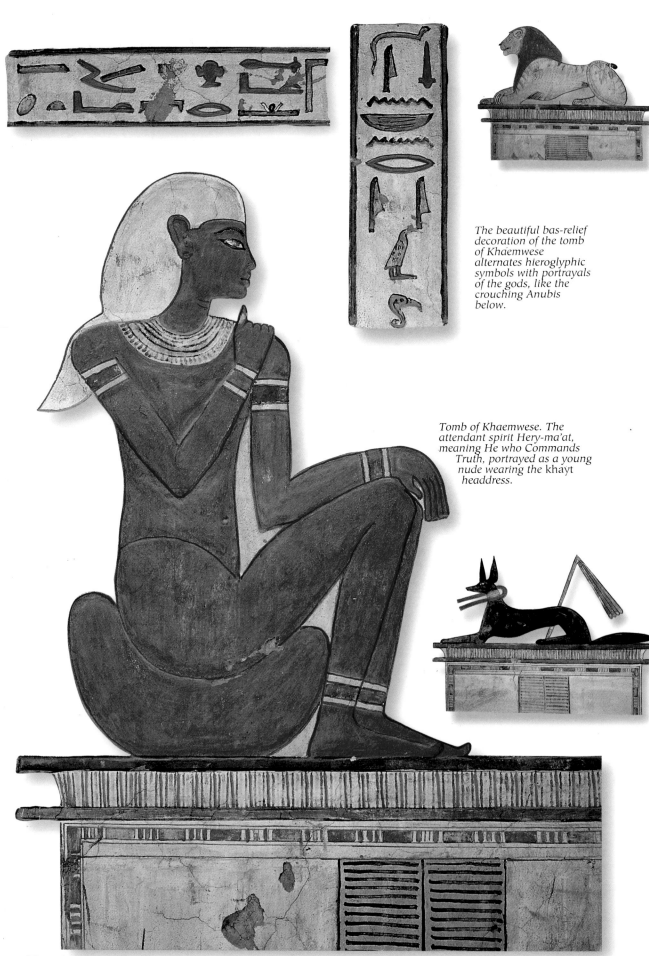

The beautiful bas-relief decoration of the tomb of Khaemwese alternates hieroglyphic symbols with portrayals of the gods, like the crouching Anubis below.

Tomb of Khaemwese. The attendant spirit Hery-ma'at, meaning He who Commands Truth, portrayed as a young nude wearing the khayt headdress.

MEDINET HABU

For a long time, Medinet Habu was considered nothing more than a rich quarry where large ready-dressed stones could be found. In Christian times, a village rose and occupied most of the temple area - which the Copts called the Mound of Djeme - and in this case, the new utilization resulted in saving many remains which otherwise would have been lost.

The massive pylon of the facade of the temple and a detail of the bas-reliefs celebrating the victories of Ramses III.

One of the plates drawn during the French-Tuscan expedition led by Jean-François Champollion and Ippolito Rosellini, showing Ramses III defeating his enemies and subjugating the foreign peoples.

On the following pages, a reconstruction and an example of the abundant decoration of the Temple of Medinet Habu.

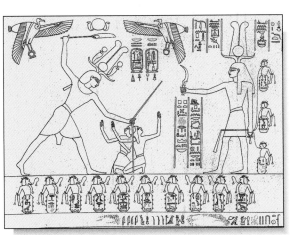

Excavations have brought to light the traces of an entire city around the pharaoh's palace, but only one home has been found: that of an overseer of the necropolis.

The monumental complex of Medinet Habu includes the **Temple of Ramses III**, preceded by the **shrine of Thutmose I** and the chapels of the adoring divinities of Amon. Formidable, almost military in appearance, is the fine **Southern Gate**, set between two towers.

Above it open the two rows of longitudinal windows of the Royal Pavilion. The "martial" aspect of this construction is further emphasized by the bas-reliefs on the walls of the towers: sacrifices of prisoners, the pharaoh leading captured enemies to the god Amon, and so on.

From the point of view of style, the **Temple of Ramses III** is one of the most perfect buildings in all Egyptian art. A pylon 63 meters wide, decorated with scenes of war, leads to a **first court** with a gallery of Osiris pillars on the east side.

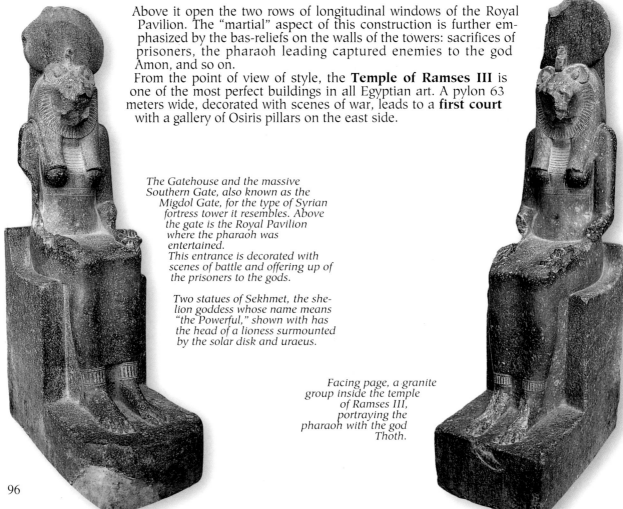

The Gatehouse and the massive Southern Gate, also known as the Migdol Gate, for the type of Syrian fortress tower it resembles. Above the gate is the Royal Pavilion where the pharaoh was entertained.
This entrance is decorated with scenes of battle and offering up of the prisoners to the gods.

Two statues of Sekhmet, the she-lion goddess whose name means "the Powerful," shown with has the head of a lioness surmounted by the solar disk and uraeus.

Facing page, a granite group inside the temple of Ramses III, portraying the pharaoh with the god Thoth.

Thirty-eight lines of hieroglyphs on the second pylon of the temple narrate the military exploits of Ramses III.

On the right tower is the celebration of the pharaoh's victory, in the eighth year of his reign, over the powerful coalition of the neighboring Libyan tribes and the so-called Sea Peoples, a confederation including the Danuna, the Akawasha, the Luka, and the Tjekker (the Danaoi, Achaeans, Lycians, and Teucri of Greek fame), probably all Indo-European peoples who had represented a menace for Egypt since the time of Merneptah.

Ramses III, with an able strategic maneuver, succeeded in stymieing the invaders on the Delta by deploying archers on the banks and a blockade of ships on the river.

The enemy ships were sunk and the survivors had little choice but to flee.

Left, bottom of page, an architrave of the temple with the goddess Nekhbet portrayed in vulture form.

The first courtyard of the Temple of Ramses III is delimited on the right by seven Osiris pillars and on the left by eight papyrus columns with open papyrus capitals.

Other pylons and other courts lead to the last hypostyle hall, dominated by a statuary group of Ramses III with the god Thoth. But not all the decorations in the temple of Medinet Habu are military in character: in an architrave, for example, the goddess Nekhbet is shown as a vulture protecting Upper Egypt and, symbolically, the grandiose temple complex.

THE VALLEY OF THE ARTISANS

A few kilometers south of Sheikh Abd el-Qurna is the valley now known as Deir el-Medina ("the Monastery of the Town" in Arabic), after a monastery that stood here during the Coptic period.

The "town" is the ruined Workmen's Village, begun under Thutmose I and inhabited through the five centuries of activity of the valley, from 1550 to 1000 BC, by the craftsmen who built and decorated the royal tombs of Thebes. They were stone cutters, masons, painters, and sculptors, who every morning traveled the steep path over the harsh hills around Deir el-Bahari to the royal necropolis; the children and the women instead stayed at the village, where they cultivated wheat and barley. The workers labored at the royal necropolis eight hours a day for nine consecutive days, and on the tenth - the day of rest - they decorated their own tombs. The teams of artisans (called Servants of the Place of Truth) were directed by several overseers and were divided into two groups: those who worked on the right walls and those who worked on the left walls. As adepts of the royal tombs, these workers were considered "holders of secrets" and therefore subject to living surrounded by walls.

The houses were small and very simple: built one next to the other, in mudbrick, whitewashed inside. Generally, they consisted of a tiny entrance, a reception room, a second room, and the kitchen; sometimes, but infrequently, they also had a cellar and a terrace. Nothing remains of whatever decoration they might have had.

The necropolis is on the west side of the valley; the tombs are all alike, consisting of a chapel and a small, painted subterranean room.

Aerial view of the Workmen's Village. The necropolis extended along the slopes west of the village walls.

The Tomb of Pashed

This tomb, from the Ramesside era, is located high up in the central sector of the necropolis.

A steep staircase leads to the subterranean apartment, in which an unadorned antechamber precedes the burial chamber, with its mudbrick walls covered with stucco and painted with tempera. Pashed is shown with his wife Nediem-behedet and his sons, and is referred to as a Servant of the Place of Truth; that is, a simple construction worker at the royal necropolis. As an older man, Pashed was perhaps promoted to the post of foreman. Only recently opened to visitors, the tomb is of interest not only for the lively, brilliant colors of its wall decorations, but also for the spiritual and religious significance of the verses of the *Book of the Dead* (*Am-Tuat*) they contain.

Tomb of Pashed. Top, a painting on the east wall, south of the door, showing various figures at the funeral rites for Pashed: Pashed's father Menna, his mother Hut, and Nefersekheru, a friend of the deceased.

Right, the goddess Hathor and the ibis-headed god Thoth as painted on the north vault of the tomb; the east wall of the burial chamber is decorated with a depiction of the god Ptah in the form of a spread-winged falcon on the solar bark of the morning.

Tomb of Pashed. Osiris, his face painted green, wearing the nemes headdress, is at the center of this composition showing Horus in falcon form and the uadjet eye, from which there issues an arm holding a vase containing torches, against the backdrop of the mountain to the west of the Workmen's Village.

Two details of the painting in the lunette, shown above. Left, the deceased Pashed kneeling in adoration of the god Osiris; the inscription reads "Servant in the House of Truth." Right, the attendant spirit Teka, whose name means "torch," holds a vase containing torches to illuminate the god.

Pashed kneeling under a palm to drink the water of the Nile. The hieroglyphic text in the background is Chapter 62 of the Book of the Dead, which contains the formula that permits drinking of the Nile in the otherworld.

THE TOMB OF SENNEDJEM

In the vivacity and freshness of its decoration, the tomb of Sennedjem, Servant of the Place of Truth and an official of the necropolis in the 19th Dynasty, is perhaps the finest in the necropolis. All that remains of it is the practically-intact main burial chamber; the furnishings that it held are now on exhibit in the Egyptian Museum of Cairo.

The far wall of the tomb shows Sennedjem and his wife Iyneferti in adoration of the gods of the otherworld. In the upper register of the lunette are portrayed two Anubis' protecting the doors to the otherworld and two large uadjet eyes, symbols of the supreme god. The first god on the left in the upper line is Osiris: the green color of his skin is the symbol of the rebirth of life. Ra-Harakhte is on the left in the lower set.

Detail of the painting of Iyneferti, wife of Sennedjem. The woman's head is surmounted by a perfume cone - an emptied gourd filled with scented cream that melted at body temperature to emit a pleasing fragrance that scented hair and clothing. The flower worn by Sennedjem's wife in her hair was a customary adornment on occasion of banquets and ceremonies.

Facing page, the representation of Osiris in the tomb of Sennedjem. The god's body is wrapped in the shroud; his hands and face are painted green to symbolize the rebirth of vegetation. He holds the crook and the flagellum, symbols of royal power, and on his head wears the atef crown of braided rushes and feathers around the solar disk. To the sides of Osiris are two fetishes of Anubis, represented by two pelts hanging from staffs.

The decoration of one wall of the tomb of Sennedjem provides us with a precious illustration one of the most important moments in the Egyptian funeral rite. The priest, wearing the mask of Anubis, the protector god of the necropolises, touches the heart and the stomach of the mummy to awaken him and accompany him into the next life. In place of the heart he will set a scarab amulet, with the formulas of the *Book of the Dead* inscribed on its back.

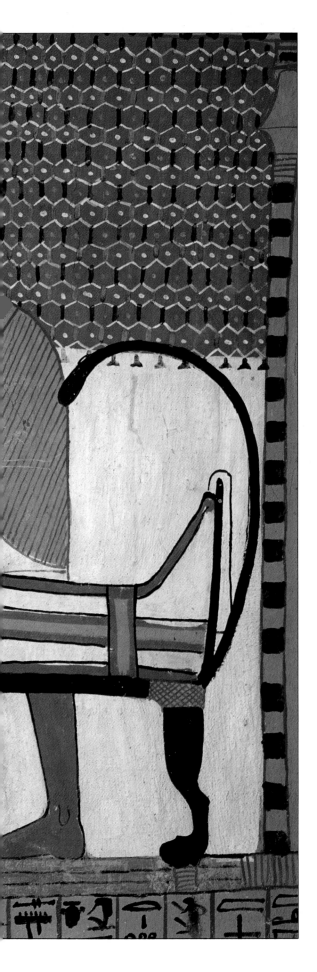

MUMMIFICATION RITES

The perfect embalming techniques used by the ancient Egyptians are believed to be only secondarily responsible for the spectacular state of preservation of the corpses; the principal reason would appear to be the extremely dry climate of Egypt and the total absence of bacteria in the air and the sand.

Just how was a corpse mummified? The body of the deceased was entrusted to the hands of specialists, who began the embalming by using a hook to extract the brain through the nostrils. The skull was then filled with a mixture based on liquid bitumen, which hardened as it cooled. The eyes were removed and later replaced with enameled orbs. Using an extremely sharp stone, an incision was made on the left side of the body and the viscera were extracted. Only the heart was left in place. After being treated with boiling bitumen, the stomach, liver, lungs, and intestines were wrapped and then sealed in four canopic jars of clay, limestone, alabaster, other stones, or metal, depending on the social standing of the dead man; the heads figured on the stoppers of the single jars - one human, one a jackal, one a hawk, and one a baboon - symbolized the four attendant spirits of the dead. The jars were placed together in a single container, near the mummy.

The interior cavities of the corpse were carefully washed with palm wine, dried using a powder of aromatic plants, and finally filled with ground myrrh or with perfumed wood sawdust. Thus prepared, the body was immersed in a bath of natron (natural sodium carbonate) for seventy days. At the end of this period, during which the fleshy parts dissolved in the natron solution, all that remained was the skin attached to the bones. The hair of the men was cut short, while that of the women was left in all its splendid length.

At this point, the corpse was wrapped with narrow bindings impregnated with resin on the lower side; wrapping began with the separate fingers, then the hand, and finally the arm; then the foot and leg, and so on. Work on the head was more meticulous. A cloth similar to muslin was used in immediate contact with the skin. The figure was covered with several layers of bindings, which adhered so perfectly that if they had been removed all together, a plaster cast made from them would have been an exact portrait of the dead man. The entire body, lying supine, with the hands crossed on the breast or with the arms stretched out along the sides, was then again wrapped in bindings for its entire length. The corpses of the pharaohs merited a precious shroud or a golden case on which were embossed the features of the dead man.

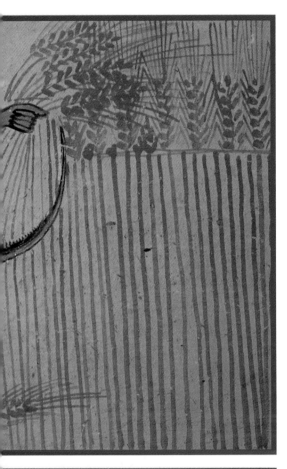

FARMING IN ANCIENT EGYPT

The book The Teachings of Amen-emhet *is attributed to Amenemhet I, founder of the 12th dynasty. In one passage of the work, the pharaoh addresses his son with the words, " . . . I cultivated the grain, I venerated the god of grain in every valley of the Nile. No one has known hunger or thirst during my reign."*

Agriculture was always one of the mainstays of the ancient Egyptian economy, and it was strictly linked to the flood cycle of the Nile river. Each year, punctually in late May or early June, the Nile flood waters arrived in Egyptian territory, submerging the fields and depositing, during the season of Akhet, or "inundation," a layer of fertile mud, which dried out by November. It was then that fieldwork began: plowing and sowing, followed by the harvest and the threshing of the grain.

Once separated from the chaff, the grain was sealed in amphorae or sacks and taken to the warehouses for storage, all under the attentive eyes of the scribes, who recorded the exact quantities.

Besides grain, other important crops were millet and barley (from which beer, the "national drink," was produced).

The Egyptians also harvested the papyrus, which was used for making ropes, sandals, and boats - but most importantly, it was cut into thin strips, beaten, and woven to produce sheets for writing and painting.

Two scenes of rural life which at the same time possess deep religious significance. Sennedjem and his wife are at work in the fields, where they plow with two pied heifers and sow and reap the grain with the typical Egyptian scythe with its short wooden handle and flint blade. The fields are lined with date palms, sycamores, and dum palms. Symbolically, the painting represents the tilling of the Fields of Iaru, the Elysian Fields of ancient Egypt, where Osiris reigned supreme as king. Once justified and absolved, the dead could accede to this realm and continue an existence similar to that conducted on earth, working in the fields.

THE TOMB OF INHERKHA

Under Ramses III and Ramses IV, Inherkha held the office of Vice Master of the Double Land of the Place of Truth; he was, in other words, a foreman, entrusted with coordinating the work of the laborers working under his direction. He had two tombs built for himself, but only the one lower down the slope, closer to the village, has lively, imaginative decoration.

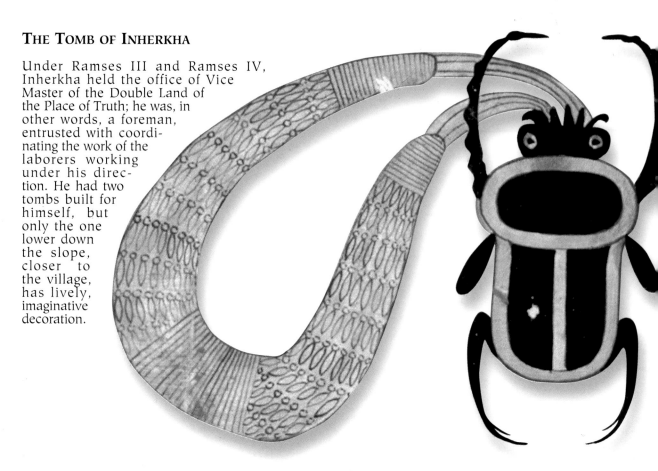

Top, a painting in the tomb of Inherka showing the scarab alongside the necklace of Hathor; bottom, three jackal-headed spirits.

On the next page, two more details of the pictorial decoration of the tomb of Inherka: a procession and the solar bark navigating on the Nile of the otherworld, with aboard the dead Inherka with Isis, Thoth, Khepri, and Hu.

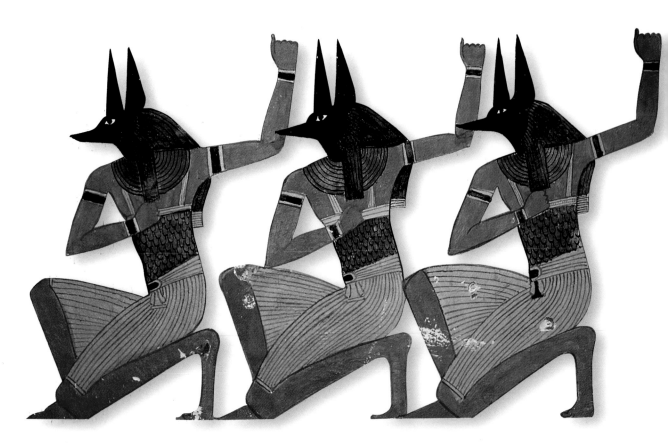

Again in the tomb of Inherka, the elegant stride of four tall, slender jackals towing the solar bark.

A stucco painting in the tomb of Ipuy illustrates a scene of fishermen net-fishing from a light papyrus boat.

THE TOMB OF IPUY

Ipuy, a sculptor under Ramses II, had his tomb decorated with unusual and curious scenes: even if the style is rather sketchy, the wealth of details (for example, the oculist putting drops into the eyes of a patient) is such as to make this one of the best-known tombs in the necropolis.

THE TEMPLE OF DEIR EL-MEDINA

The Small Temple at Deir el-Medina, dedicated to the deities of the necropolis, Hathor and Ma'at, was begun by Ptolemy IV Philopator and completed under Euergetes II; later in history it was occupied by Christian monks. The temple has come down to us complete with its enclosing walls and the storehouses. On the rear wall, decorated near the top with seven masks of Hathor, there open three chapels with beautiful ornamental reliefs.

The plain facade of the Ptolemaic Temple of Deir el-Medina; in the inset, David Roberts' rendition of the temple.

Deir el-Medina and History's First Strike

What we might call the first workers' strike in history occurred during the twenty-ninth year of the reign of Ramses III. The craftsmen of Deir el-Medina involved in the construction and decoration of the tombs in the Valley of the Kings, having for some time not received their salaries (consisting of lengths of cloth, bread, and jars of oil and fat), simply set down their tools. They went to the Temple of Thutmose III, where they complained to the Vizier, "We have come here driven by hunger and thirst. We have no clothes; we have neither oil nor fish nor legumes . . ."
The Vizier offered his guarantee that the pharaoh's promises would be fulfilled and convinced the laborers to take up work again.
Not long afterwards, payments were again suspended. The workers went out on strike again, but this time they occupied the Mortuary Temple of Ramses III and sacked it, carrying off the furnishings.

Egyptian Museum, Turin. The "Papyrus of the Workmen's Strike."

THE VALLEY OF THE NOBLES

Compared with the tombs of the pharaohs, those of the high dignitaries of the Middle Kingdom dynasties are architecturally extremely simple. They all have the same layout: an open-air terrace, followed by a vestibule with painted walls illustrating the terrestrial occupations of the owner and a corridor leading to a niche where a statue of the deceased, sometimes together with those of his wife or relatives, is often found. The paintings in these tombs are characterized by freshness and vivacity and an unusual realism, and bear witness to the life at court in ancient Egypt. The most frequent subjects are funeral banquets (with music and dance), work in the fields, crafts activities, and scenes of daily life in general.

THE TOMB OF SENEFER

A flight of 43 steps cut into the rock takes us into the lovely tomb of Senefer, prince of the Southern City (Thebes) and Superintendent of the Granaries and Livestock of Amon under Amenhotep II.
The anonymous painter of this tomb decorated the ceiling with a marvelous pergola of purple grapes.

Two details of the decoration of the tomb of Senefer, showing the deceased with his wife Seth-Nefer , a royal nurse, and with their daughter Mutahi, depicted - as was customary - as a small figure at her father's knee during a banquet.

114

THE TOMB OF RAKH-MARA

This tomb, which structurally could be taken as an example of a Theban civilian tomb of the 18th Dynasty, belonged to Rakh-Mara (or Rekhmire), Viceroy and Governor of Thebes and vizier under Thutmose III and Amenhotep II. Both the vestibule and the chapel are decorated; besides being utterly beautiful, the paintings are of immense historical interest since they provide invaluable illustrations, in a great number of scenes, of Egypt's relations with other countries at the time. The liveliest depictions are those in which representatives of foreign countries bring their offerings: the emissaries of the land of Punt (Somalia), carrying ebony, ivory, and ostrich feathers, are clearly identifiable; likewise those of the land of Kefti (perhaps Crete) with their curly hair and long braids on their breasts. Then there are the black Africans of Kush, dressed in panther skins, who bring a jaguar, a giraffe, and monkeys, and the ambassadors of the land of Retenu (Syrians and Assyrians), who lead two horses, a bear, and an elephant.

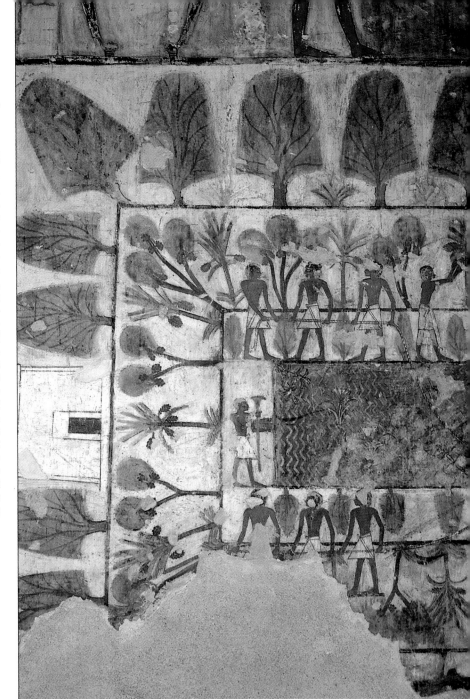

Tomb of Rakh-Mara. Top, a detail of the garden centering on the pool with its waters rippled by the wind and showing gardeners caring for the fruit trees.
Bottom, the princes of Crete carrying precious vases as gifts to Rakh-Mara; craftsmen at work.

On the left wall of the
corridor in the tomb of
Rakh-Mara, a group of
workers sculpt a colossal
statue of a pharaoh.
Beginning in New
Kingdom times, the
construction of colossi
portraying the reigning
pharaoh became a booming
business.
Scaffolding permitted the
sculptors to work around the
huge blocks of stone that made
up the images of the pharaohs.
Different workers had different
specialties: one sanded the
chisel-finished surfaces,
another polished, another
added the final touches.

Tomb of Userhet. From the Old Kingdom onward, it was customary for the Egyptians to shave their faces completely, even though the nobility often wore thin mustaches. The beard was allowed to grow only during mourning. The figure of the barber was a popular one; his tools were a low stool, on which the customer sat, and a recipient containing his razor (a simple flint blade - which later evolved to bronze - with a wooden handle).
When the customer was a noble or an aristocrat, the barber was summoned to the palace or richly-appointed home to render his services.

THE TOMB OF USERHET

Userhet, a royal scribe under Amenophis II, had his tomb built and decorated with paintings which are still extraordinarily well preserved today. The unusual scene of a barber shaving his customer in a garden is famous.

The Tomb of Khaemhet

Khaemhet, also known as Mahu, was a royal scribe and Inspector of the Granaries of Upper and Lower Egypt under Amenophis III. His tomb, decorated with elegant bas-reliefs, is at the back of a courtyard overlooked by other tombs of the period. The niche in the burial chamber, which is deeply excavated into the rock, contains the statues of the deceased and his relatives, divided into three groups.

Tomb of Khaemhet. The statues, unfortunately in poor condition, of Khaemhet and his relative Imhotep, a royal scribe, in a niche in the first large chamber of the tomb.

On the page to the left, two more images of the tomb of Userhet:
a group of servants paying homage to their master; below, men pulling a chariot by the harness and leading a horse by the reins (the upper register illustrates the storehouses in which provisions were kept).

Tomb of Userhet: the depiction of a ship with the pilot bridge at the prow.

Tomb of Userhet: a scene of the grape harvest. Right, the gathering of the grapes and, left, the harvest being packed in amphorae and recorded.

Tomb of Neferhabef: two priests making libations and offers. The effeminate features are reminiscent of Amarnian art.

The Tomb of Neferhabef

Neferhabef, also called Userhet, was the First Prophet of the Royal *Ka* of Thutmose I at the time of the pharaoh Seti I. The goddess Isis appears in the decoration of the first room, in the form of a sycamore tree that nourishes the family of the deceased. The sycamore, together with the date palm, was the sacred tree which symbolized universal power and, as such, was associated with the cosmic goddesses Isis, Nut, and Hathor.

THE TOMB OF RAMOSE

The tomb of Ramose, Governor of Thebes and vizier under Amenhotep III and later Akhenaton, is a splendid example of the delicate moment of transition in Egyptian art toward the new Amarna style.

The tomb was never finished, since during its construction the capital was moved from Thebes to Amarna, but the decoration - mostly bas-relief - is nevertheless sufficient to illustrate the refined lifestyle of Ramose and his wife.

One of the most striking works is the scene of the newlyweds at table, dressed in light linen tunics and wearing heavy wigs arranged in ringlets. Like other everyday objects, the wig also evolved through history: from simple and straight in the Old Kingdom, it became more elaborate and voluminous with time.

Tomb of Ramose. The hypostyle hall is the only decorated portion; on the south side is the famous scene of Ramose's funeral procession, which, thanks to its wealth of precise detail regarding the ceremony is considered one of the finest examples of Egyptian funerary art.

The servants are carrying furniture: a bed with headrest, four tabernacle-shaped containers holding the possessions of the deceased, a chair with legs in the form of lion's paws, vases containing unguents and scented oils. They are followed by others carrying amphorae and flowers; in their midst, the group of weepers, who, with their tresses unbound in sign of mourning and with their arms upraised, keen laments and cries of sorrow for the death of Ramose. The weepers were hired mourners who were present at all the funeral ceremonies.

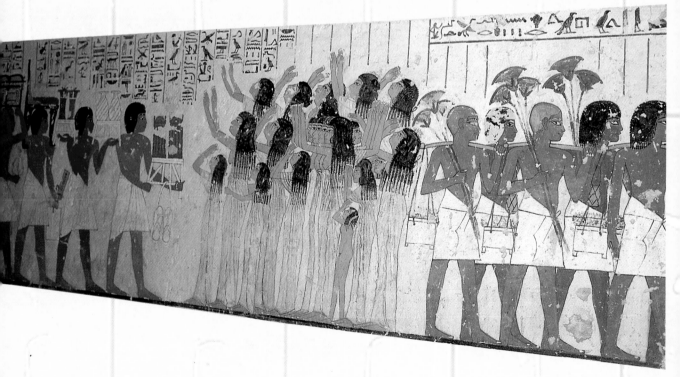

On these pages, images from the tomb of Nakht.
Above, a kneeling servant with flowers and a vine-
shoot laden with bunches of grapes.
On the facing page, two scenes of fieldwork. Top, the
cut spikes are collected in large net sacks. Bottom,
farmers use special winnowing implements to throw
the spikes in the air to separate the grain from the
chaff.

124

THE TOMB OF NAKHT

This tomb, typical of the 18th Dynasty, is one of the best preserved tombs in the necropolis. The owner was a scribe and astronomer of Amon in the time of Thutmose IV, while his wife was a singer of Amon. In the time of Akhenaton's heresy, the name of Amon was systematically scraped out of all the inscriptions. The aspect of the tomb is that of a classical hypogeum; the accurately-executed decoration is found only in the transverse vestibule.

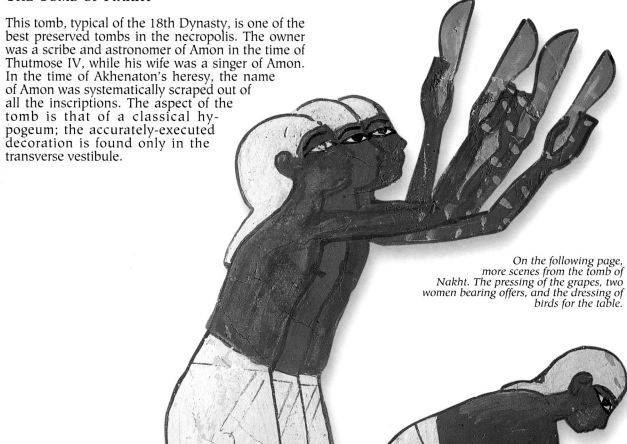

On the following page, more scenes from the tomb of Nakht. The pressing of the grapes, two women bearing offers, and the dressing of birds for the table.

125

THE TOMB OF MENNA

The owner of this tomb was Menna, scribe of the Land Registry under Thutmose IV. To create it, he requisitioned - and enlarged - an earlier tomb. The brilliant paintings that embellish its walls with detailed, lively scenes are generally considered to be among the most elegant compositions in the whole necropolis. The many subjects depicted include the hunt, offerings, and work in the fields.

Tomb of Menna. Two girls dresses in light linen tunics. The first carries a perfume vase and two bunches of flowers.

On the page to the left, top, offer-bearers painted on the walls of the tomb of Menna; bottom, detail of a painting of Menna hunting in the swamps, showing his daughter seated between his legs.

Tomb of Menna. Scene of a reception in Menna's home, with a woman offering a necklace to the couple; bottom, offer-bearers.

THE TOMB OF NEBAMUN AND IPUKY

This tomb was prepared for two sculptors, both active under Amenhotep III and Amenhotep IV. Nebamun was Chief Sculptor of the Master of the Double Land; Ipuky was Sculptor of the Master of the Double Land. Known also as the tomb of the engravers, its interesting decoration shows much about how the artisans of ancient Egypt worked.

THE TOMB OF KIKI

The tomb of Kiki, a Royal Intendant, was long abandoned and even used as stables.

Its decoration is brilliant and lively in both realization and subject matter: an entire wall is given over to scenes of the journey of the dead to Abydos. All Egyptians were required to make a pilgrimage to the temple of this sacred

city, dedicated entirely to the worship of Osiris, at least once in their lifetimes. Traditionally, Abydos was sanctuary in which the head of Osiris was preserved, and the greatest wish of all religious Egyptians was to have a mortuary chapel there - or at the very least a commemorative stela.

Tomb of Kiki. Top, the journey of the boat that accompanied the deceased to Abydos, with the weepers intoning their keening laments.
Bottom, a detail of the boat and the baldachin sheltering the mummy of the deceased.

On the page to the left, top, tomb of Nebamun and Ipuky. The two deceased are purified before being sealed in the tomb; each of the mummies of the two men is preceded by a portrayal of the widow Henutnofre, who was wife to both sculptors.
Below, the tomb of Kiki. The deceased, wearing a short beard, is followed by his wife, shown holding a sistrum.

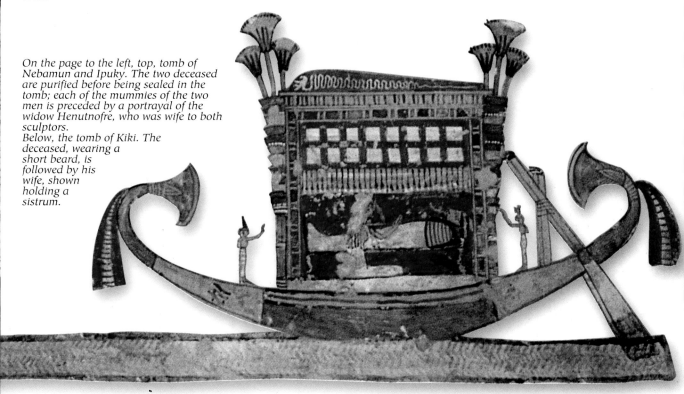

131

THE TOMB OF KHERUEF SENA'A

Kheruef Sena'a was the Intendant of the Great Royal Bride; that is, of Tiye, a Syrian princess famous for her beauty, the beloved wife of Amenhotep III and mother of Akhenaton, the heretic pharaoh.

The tomb the intendant had built is vast but unfinished. The western part of the court, with its depiction of Amenhotep III's Jubilee celebration (*Heb Sed*), is a true masterpiece.

The elegant bas-reliefs in the tomb of Kheruef Sena'a show young women engaged in conversation and dance. The typical costume of the dancers is a short skirt with crossed suspenders tied in the front so as to allow great freedom of movement. The dance shown in this tomb is that performed in celebration of the Jubilee of Amenhotep III.

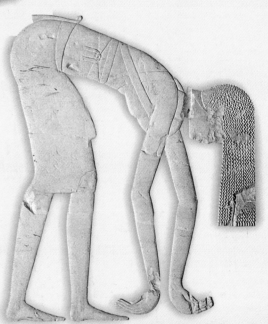

MORTUARY COMPLEX OF MENTUHOTEP

Temple of Thutmose III
Hypostyle hall
Courtyard
Pyramidal tumulus
Terrace with colonnade
Lower vestibule

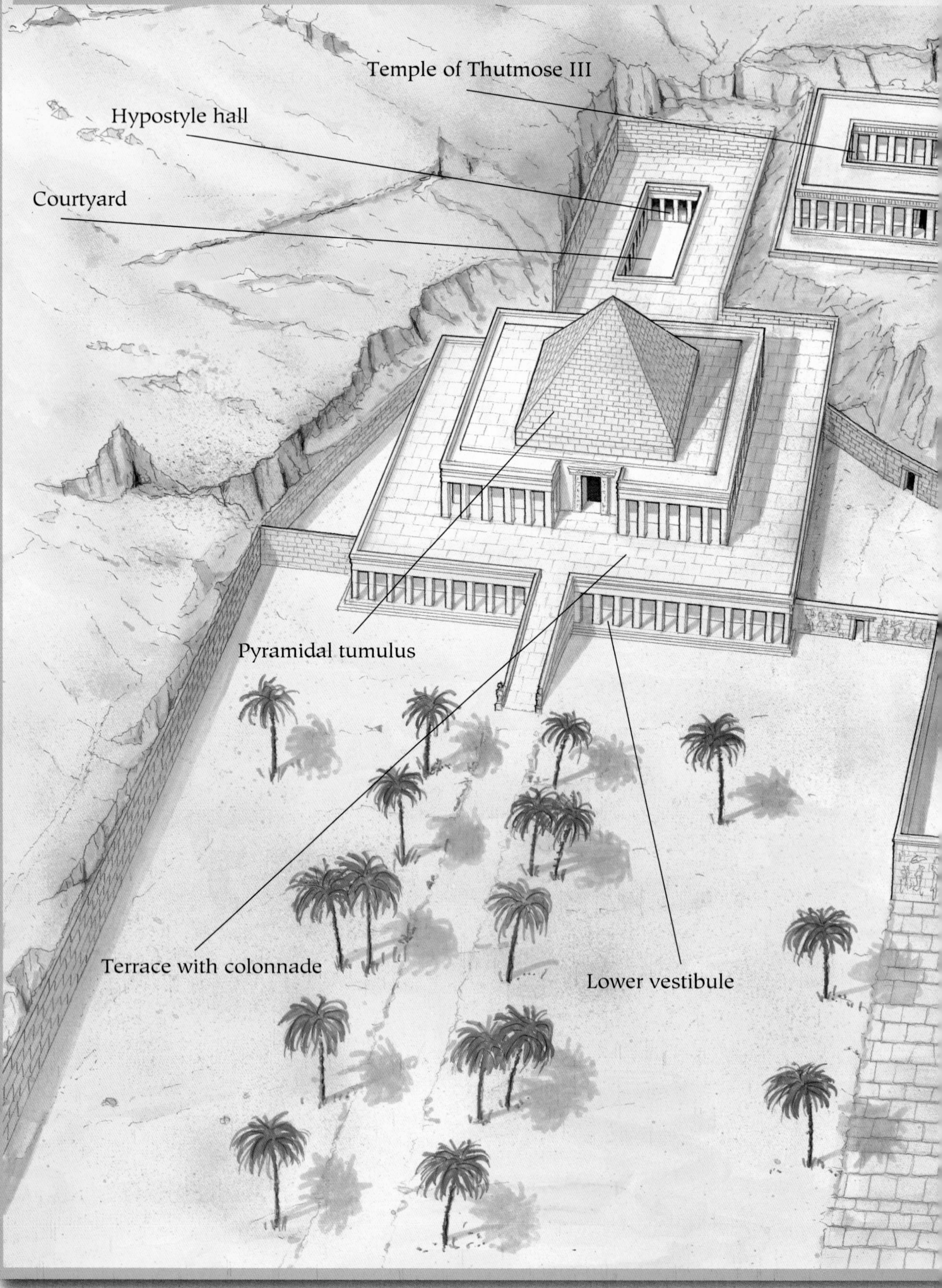

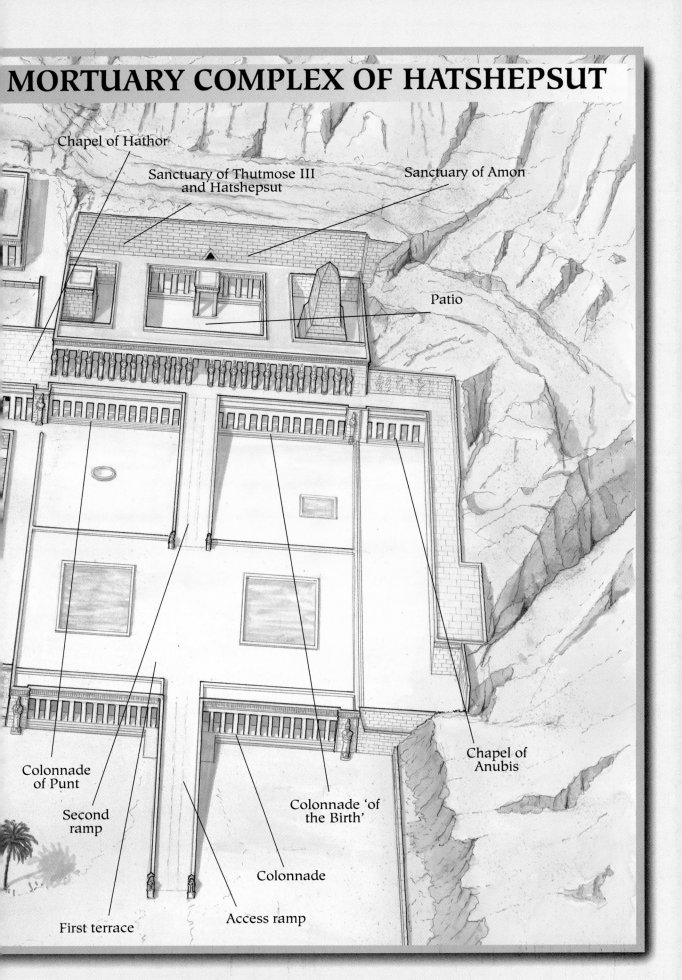

Chapel of Hathor

Sanctuary of Thutmose III and Hatshepsut

Sanctuary of Amon

Patio

Chapel of Anubis

Colonnade of Punt

Second ramp

Colonnade 'of the Birth'

Colonnade

First terrace

Access ramp

A view of the monumental complex at Deir el-Bahari and a detail of an Osiris pillar on which Hatshepsut is portrayed wearing a beard, traditionally an attribute of male royalty.

DEIR EL-BAHARI

One thousand two hundred years after Imhotep, another architect, Senmut, appeared on the scene of Egyptian history with another architectural masterpiece. Queen Hatshepsut, more a patron of the arts than a military leader, ordered a funerary monument for her father Thutmose I and for herself and chose an impervious valley already consecrated to the goddess Hathor who, in the form of a heifer, received the deceased in the afterworld. Queen Hatshepsut's monument was in later times abandoned; at a certain point in history it became a Christian convent called the Convent of the North, and this fact not only gave the area its present name of Deir el-Bahari but also preserved the Pharaonic temple from further destruction.

The famous architect and minister Senmut brilliantly exploited the dramatic fan of ochre-colored rock that stretches out behind the monument, which was built according to a new and revolutionary concept.

The east-facing **Temple of Hatshepsut**, called in antiquity Djeser-djeseru, "more splendid than splendid," is unique in Egyptian architecture. It consisted of a series of vast terraces which, via ramps, led up to the sanctuary. An avenue of sphinxes and obelisks led up to the **first terrace**, closed at the back by a portico of 22 pillars and flanked by two Osiris pillars, from which another ramp led to the **second terrace**, also equipped with a portico of two rows of square pillars. On one of the walls, beautiful bas-reliefs narrate the stories of the queen's birth and childhood and of the expedition sent by her to the mysterious land of Punt (perhaps today's Somalia, to judge from the giraffes, monkeys, panther skins, and ivory objects that are shown).

Hatshepsut, Queen and Pharaoh

At the time of Thutmose I's death, the panorama at court was quite complex. Since the two eldest sons had died, the legitimate heir to the throne was the third son, Thutmose II, who was made to marry his half-sister Hatshepsut, the eldest daughter of Thutmose I and Queen Ahmose-Nofretari.

The couple reigned jointly for a few years. Thutmose II died prematurely, leaving as heir an illegitimate son by a concubine, also named Thutmose and tagged as legitimate heir by his father, who certainly guessed at the ambitious designs of his half-sister and wife. The future Thutmose III was still a child when Hatshepsut, his stepmother and aunt, stepped into the post of regent. Hatshepsut was an intelligent woman of uncommon ability, with a keen political sense. She was also attractive, and ambitious: she wanted to be king, not a mere queen, and thus desired divine legitimation. Accordingly, she appealed to Theban religion and the clergy and orchestrated a public statement of legitimacy: the god Amon, in the likeness of the pharaoh Thutmose I, would have lain with Queen Ahmose and fathered Hatshepsut, who was therefore by divine right the "daughter of the king, sister of the king, wife of the god, and the Great Royal Wife."

At this point Hatshepsut began to assume masculine characteristics: she adopted royal protocol, wore men's clothing and the postiche beard, and suppressed the feminine endings of her names.

"Pharaoh Hatshepsut" also began dedicating her time to architecture - for example, her funeral temple at Deir el-Bahari - and to promoting new trade policy, which culminated in the expedition to the Land of Punt.

Above, the black granite cube statue of Senmut with the princess Nefrure or Nefru-Ra. Bottom, the relief, on the second southern colonnade of the temple, portraying Eti, Queen of Punt, with her generous forms bordering on the obese.

On the last wall, 18 niches, large and small, must have held just as many statues of the queen in standing and seated poses. The temple is also home to the 16-faceted **pillar** so admired for its elegance by Champollion that he called it "proto-Doric."

Although the tomb of Senmut is about 15 meters from the east corner of the first terrace, he was not buried here but at

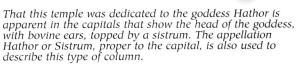

Sheikh Abd el-Qurna.

The entire left side of the valley was occupied by the gigantic **mortuary Temple of Mentuhotep II** built five hundred years before Hatshepsut decided to install hers in the same place. In the main, the tomb reflects the architectural canons typical of the Old Kingdom, but in many respects also heralds Middle Kingdom tomb structure.

That this temple was dedicated to the goddess Hathor is apparent in the capitals that show the head of the goddess, with bovine ears, topped by a sistrum. The appellation Hathor or Sistrum, proper to the capital, is also used to describe this type of column.

The monumental complex consists of a gigantic tomb with a pyramidal tumulus, at the center of which was the king's sepulcher. The **Temple of Thutmose III**, now completely in ruins, later stood between this and the top terrace of Hatshepsut's temple.

Views of the Temple of Hatshepsut. The sixteen-cornered pillar is highly reminiscent of the Doric column of Greek architecture and for this reason is often termed "proto-Doric."

Both the chapel of Hathor, on the left of the
third courtyard, and the chapel of Anubis, to
the right of same, are frescoed in vivid colors;
in both, almost every image of the Queen has
been systematically obliterated.

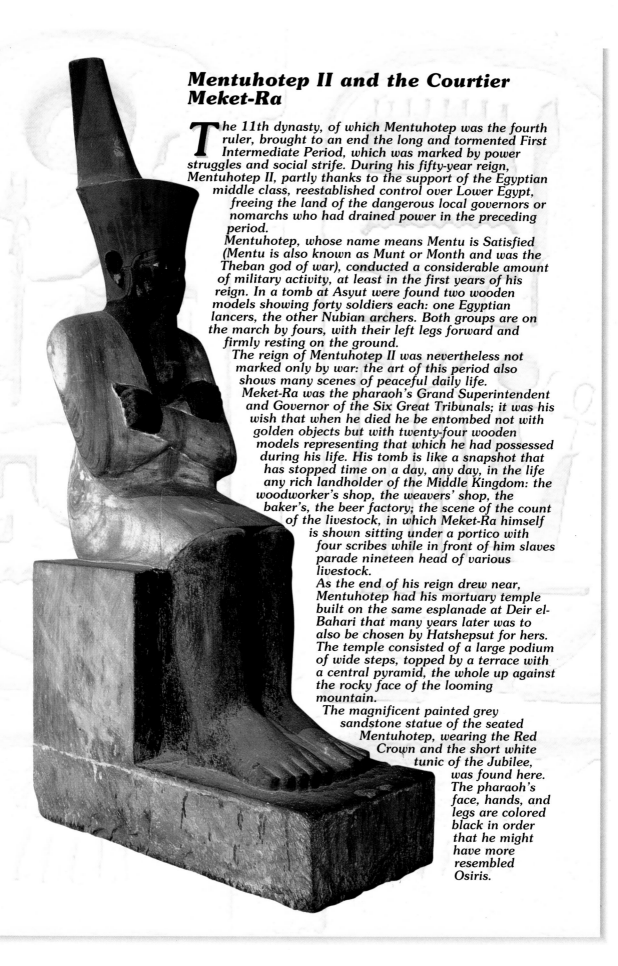

Mentuhotep II and the Courtier Meket-Ra

*T*he 11th dynasty, of which Mentuhotep was the fourth ruler, brought to an end the long and tormented First Intermediate Period, which was marked by power struggles and social strife. During his fifty-year reign, Mentuhotep II, partly thanks to the support of the Egyptian middle class, reestablished control over Lower Egypt, freeing the land of the dangerous local governors or nomarchs who had drained power in the preceding period.

Mentuhotep, whose name means Mentu is Satisfied (Mentu is also known as Munt or Month and was the Theban god of war), conducted a considerable amount of military activity, at least in the first years of his reign. In a tomb at Asyut were found two wooden models showing forty soldiers each: one Egyptian lancers, the other Nubian archers. Both groups are on the march by fours, with their left legs forward and firmly resting on the ground.

The reign of Mentuhotep II was nevertheless not marked only by war: the art of this period also shows many scenes of peaceful daily life.

Meket-Ra was the pharaoh's Grand Superintendent and Governor of the Six Great Tribunals; it was his wish that when he died he be entombed not with golden objects but with twenty-four wooden models representing that which he had possessed during his life. His tomb is like a snapshot that has stopped time on a day, any day, in the life any rich landholder of the Middle Kingdom: the woodworker's shop, the weavers' shop, the baker's, the beer factory; the scene of the count of the livestock, in which Meket-Ra himself is shown sitting under a portico with four scribes while in front of him slaves parade nineteen head of various livestock.

As the end of his reign drew near, Mentuhotep had his mortuary temple built on the same esplanade at Deir el-Bahari that many years later was to also be chosen by Hatshepsut for hers. The temple consisted of a large podium of wide steps, topped by a terrace with a central pyramid, the whole up against the rocky face of the looming mountain.

The magnificent painted grey sandstone statue of the seated Mentuhotep, wearing the Red Crown and the short white tunic of the Jubilee, was found here. The pharaoh's face, hands, and legs are colored black in order that he might have more resembled Osiris.

RAMESSEUM

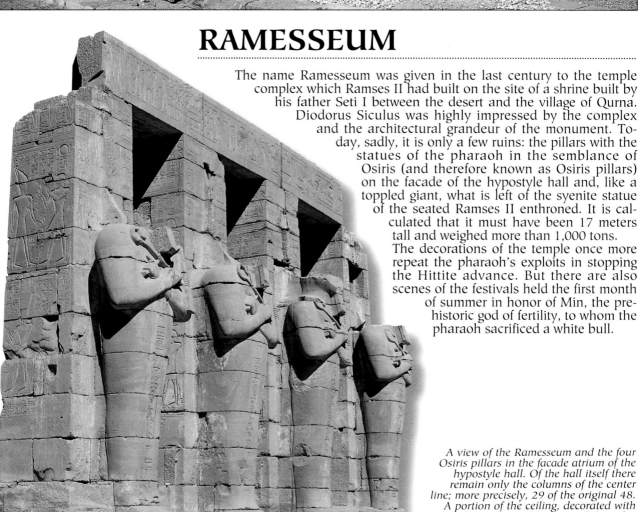

The name Ramesseum was given in the last century to the temple complex which Ramses II had built on the site of a shrine built by his father Seti I between the desert and the village of Qurna. Diodorus Siculus was highly impressed by the complex and the architectural grandeur of the monument. Today, sadly, it is only a few ruins: the pillars with the statues of the pharaoh in the semblance of Osiris (and therefore known as Osiris pillars) on the facade of the hypostyle hall and, like a toppled giant, what is left of the syenite statue of the seated Ramses II enthroned. It is calculated that it must have been 17 meters tall and weighed more than 1,000 tons.

The decorations of the temple once more repeat the pharaoh's exploits in stopping the Hittite advance. But there are also scenes of the festivals held the first month of summer in honor of Min, the prehistoric god of fertility, to whom the pharaoh sacrificed a white bull.

A view of the Ramesseum and the four Osiris pillars in the facade atrium of the hypostyle hall. Of the hall itself there remain only the columns of the center line; more precisely, 29 of the original 48. A portion of the ceiling, decorated with gold stars on a blue ground, has also been preserved.

Ramses II had no qualms about carrying off stones and decorative elements from the Temple of Hatshepsut at Deir el-Bahari to build his "Castle of a Million Years." But then, some years later, it was Ramses III who carried off material from the Ramesseum for the construction of his own temple at Medinet Habu.

When David Roberts painted the Ramesseum, the statue of Ramses II lay broken on the ground. Jean-François Champollion said of this temple that it was "perhaps the noblest and purest to be found in Thebes."

In the customary dedicatory inscription, Ramses II claimed he had built " . . this grand nave with great flowered columns . . ." The hypostyle hall of the Ramesseum was structurally quite similar to that of Karnak, with the columns of the center nave being higher than those of the aisles.

The Ramesseum was not only Ramses II's "Castle of a Million Years." It was also the headquarters from which the pharaoh's possessions were administered and a culturally active center that attracted theologians and scholars.

The head of the colossus of Ramses II.

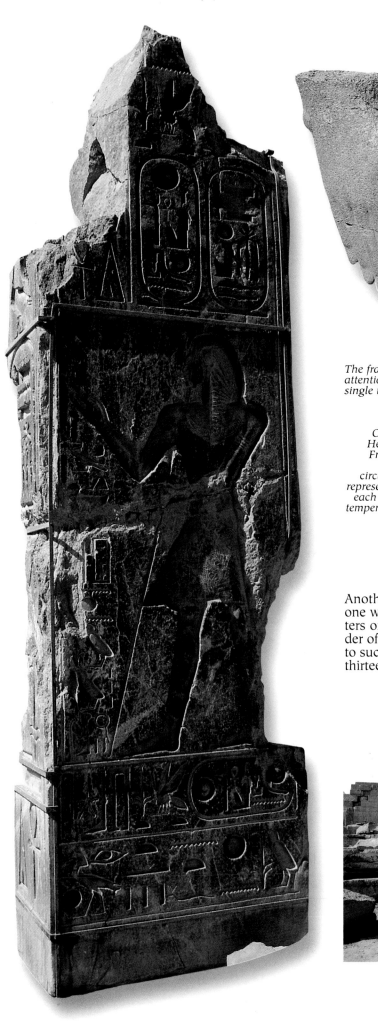

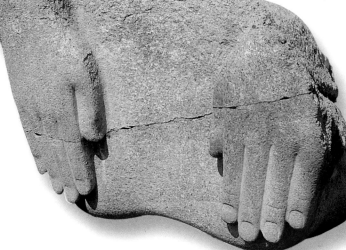

The fragments of the colossus of Ramses II show how much attention was paid to detail despite its exceptional size (a single toenail measures 19 centimeters!).

On the page to the right, the Ramesseum as painted by Hector Horeau. If this was the tomb of Ozymandias, the French artist observed, the terrace must have lodged the famous gold astronomical circle, 165 meters in circumference and divided into 365 wedges in which were represented the times of the rising and setting of the stars for each day of the year and forecasts concerning variations in temperature and the influences of the constellations on those born on each day.

Another interesting and unusual decoration is on one wall of the hypostyle hall: the sons and daughters of Ramses, in a double row, are lined up in order of succession and of birth. Merneptah, who was to succeed Ramses II on the Egyptian throne, is in thirteenth place.

Ozymandias - Belzoni the Giant and Shelley the Poet

It was Johann Ludwig Burckhardt who, during an excursion on the western bank of the Nile at Thebes, discovered the colossal remains of what was called "the young Memnon." Burckhardt would have liked to carry off the torso, but he had not the necessary means to do so; he thus called on Giovanni Battista Belzoni, the physically enormous archaeologist-adventurer from Padua and introduced him to Henry Salt, the English consul in Cairo, engaged in collecting antiquities for the British Museum, who procured the needed permits for Belzoni. On 30 June 1816, the Italian and his wife Sara left Cairo for Thebes, with only scarce equipment: four ropes made of palm leaves, four rollers, and fourteen levers, of which eight were to be used for building a sort of harness for the bust.

The work involved was far from simple: Belzoni had to act quickly, for the Nile was scheduled to reach the correct level at the temple in less than a month's time and delay would have meant waiting another year; he had to face daily struggles with the local authorities, who instigated the peasants against working for "those Christian dogs;" to further complicate matters, the feast of Ramadan fell in exactly that period. Finally, in the suffocating heat and having traveled at a rate of less than 100 meters per day, the head reached the banks of the Nile on 10 August. But there were no boats on the river, so the expedition had to wait until October for an enormous barge to arrive; this time, 130 men hefted the bust on board. It traveled from Thebes to Cairo, from Cairo via Rosetta to Alexandria, and finally on to London, where it arrived in early January 1817.

Percy Bysse Shelley had not yet seen the statue of Ramses II when he wrote his famous sonnet "Ozymandias;" rather, his inspiration came from the Classical aura of the ruins of the statue, since he never visited the site.

I met a traveler from an antique land
Who said: "Two vast and trunkless legs of stone
Stand in the desert . . . Near them, on the sand,
Half sunk, a shattered visage lies . . .
And on the pedestal these words appear:
'My name is Ozymandias, king of kings:
Look on my works, ye Mighty, and despair!'
Nothing beside remains. Round the decay
Of that colossal wreck, boundless and bare
The Lone and Level sands stretch far away."

The moving of the bust of Ramses II as imagined by Belzoni in a watercolor which later became the basis for an edition of mass-produced lithographs.

THE TOMB OF AY

The tomb of Ay, successor to Tutankhamen, is located in a ravine at the west end of the west Valley of the Kings, called by the inhabitants of the region Gabannet el-Gurud, the "cemetery of the monkeys." The tomb itself, discovered by Belzoni in 1816, is similarly called Turbet el-Gurud, "tomb of the monkeys," probably on account of the many depictions of this animal it contains. Ay's granite sarcophagus, found in pieces and patiently restored, is quite similar to that of Tutankhamen, with four spread-winged goddesses watching over the pharaoh's repose.

The interior of the tomb of Ay, with the sarcophagus and the wall paintings illustrating scenes from the Am-Tuat, *the pharaoh with the gods, and the twelve baboons that correspond to the twelve hours of the night.*

THE MORTUARY TEMPLE OF SETI I

Consecrated to the god Amon, the temple was begun by Seti I and completed by Seti's son Ramses II, who is also responsible for the sumptuous decoration. Although, unfortunately, the temple has come down to us partially destroyed, the beauty of its reliefs is on a par with Abydos.

The vestibule still contains nine of the ten original bundled papyrus columns with closed capitals. In the hypostyle hall there instead remain six, with reliefs of the two pharaohs bearing offerings to Amon. The chapels on the far side of the hall are decorated with reliefs of Seti and his *ka*, Thoth, and Osiris; the sanctuary that housed the sacred bark is likewise beautifully decorated.

On the page to the left:

Top, the ruins of the mortuary Temple of Seti I provide the background for a group gathered around a water-pipe, in a painting by David Roberts.

Bottom, a detail of the facade of the temple, with its nine papyrus columns.

This page:
Top, a view of the vestibule of the temple, showing a fascicled papyrus column with closed papyrus capital; bottom, a wall of the interior courtyard, adorned with bas-reliefs, behind the altar to the sun at the center of the space.

Some of the elegant bas-relief work on the pilasters of the sanctuary, which depict ritual scenes of worship and offerings to the gods.

Bottom, the facade of the mortuary Temple of Seti I as it is today, and the same temple in a drawing made by Karl Lepsius in November of 1844.
The German scholar headed the important expedition to Egypt sponsored by the king of Prussia from 1842 to 1845.
Thus, like Champollion had published his Monuments d'Egypte et de Nubie, *upon his return home Lepsius published his 12-volume* Denkmäler aus Aegypten und Aethiopien.

THE COLOSSI
OF MEMNON

In the vast plain that stretches out around western Thebes, between the Nile and the Valley of the Kings, are the remains of the monumental road which led to the mortuary Temple of Amenhotep III. The temple, unfortunately, has disappeared - what remains is commonly known by the name of Colossi of Memnon. These two gigantic statues (20 meters high, their feet alone measuring two meters in length and 1 meter in thickness), cut in monolithic blocks of sandstone, represent the pharaoh seated on a throne, with his hands resting on his knees. The southern colossus is considerably damaged but is in slightly better shape than the other, of which a legend recounts how in 27 BC a terrible earthquake seriously damaged almost all the monuments of Thebes and opened an enormous crack on the colossus from the top halfway to the ground before it toppled over.

It was noted that every morning, at sunrise, the statue emitted a prolonged, indistinct sound, which to some travelers seemed like a sad but harmonious song. Great historians such as Strabo, Pausanias, Tacitus, Lucian, and Philostratus corroborated the fact - and the Greek poets soon turned it into a fine legend.

The "singing stone," they said, was Memnon, the mythical son of Aurora and Tithonus and king of Egypt and Ethiopia. Sent by his father to aid Troy, besieged by the Greek army, Memnon covered himself with glory, killing Antilochus son of Nestor, in battle, but in turn he fell under the vengeful hand of Achilles. Aurora appealed in tears to Jove to have her son resuscitated at least once a day.

Thus, every morning, as Aurora caresses her son with her rays, he answers his inconsolable mother with protracted lamentations . . .

Despite the legend, the phenomenon can be scientifically explained.

The sounds were due to vibrations produced in the broken surfaces by the brusque passage from the cold of the night to the warmth of the first rays of the sun. Over the course of the centuries, the legs of the colossus have accumulated engraved epigrams and other, sometimes quite curious, inscriptions.

Details of the Colossi of Memnon. On the following page, all the grandeur of the Colossi of Memnon in images showing how they appear today and how they were rendered, rising above the Nile in flood, by David Roberts.

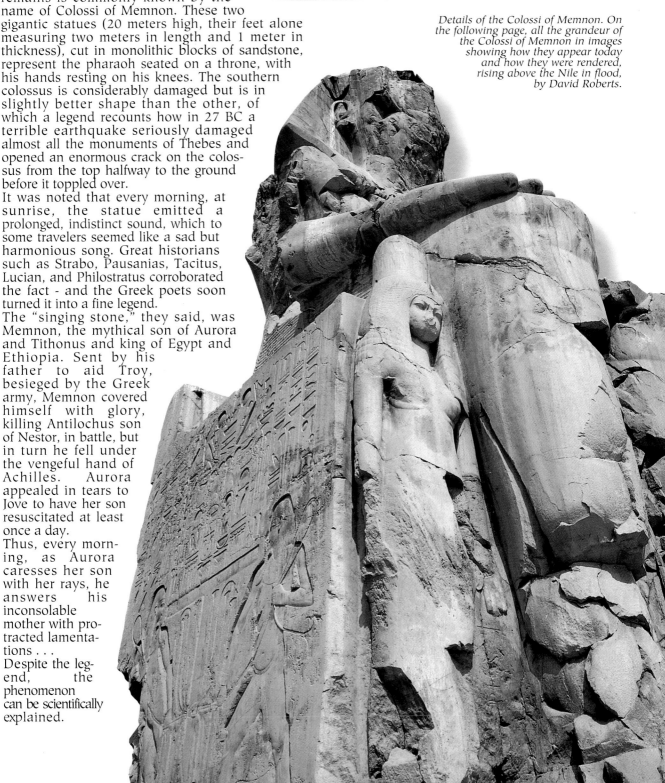

COLOSSI OF MEMNON

Seated colossi of
the pharaoh

Access pylon to the mortuary
Temple of Amenhotep III

Statue of Mutemuya,
mother of the pharaoh

Royal symbols

THE OBELISKS: FROM THE BANKS OF THE

*T*he obelisk (diminutive of the Greek **obelòs** = spit) is one of the most characteristic forms in Egyptian art and is strictly linked to worship of the sun god. The ancient Egyptians believed that the on tip of the obelisk, or pyramidon, *there alighted the phoenix, the mythical bird reborn from the ashes of its funeral pyre and whose Egyptian name* bennu *recalls the Egyptian word for the monolith,* benben.

Raised in front of the first pylon of the temple, as in Luxor, or in the interior courtyards, as in Karnak, the obelisks were majestic tributes, gifts, votive offerings made by the pharaohs to Amon-Ra.

Thutmose I, Hatshepsut, Thutmose III , and above all Ramses II competed in erecting monuments to the god. Thus, while Hat-

shepsut had erected four in Karnak, her successor erected at least nine, four of which at Karnak and two at Heliopolis - but Ramses II outdid them all: in Tanis alone he raised twenty-three.

With the Roman conquest, the obelisk lost its original, quite real religious significance and became a mere symbol. The Roman emperors saw it as a symbol of imperial greatness - and lost no time in carrying the spires off from Egypt.

Today, Egyptian obelisks are found throughout the world: in Place de la Concorde in Paris and in Central Park in New York, on the Thames in London, in the Hippodrome square in Istanbul, and in Florence's Boboli Gardens - but the

Paris, Place de la Concorde.

Rome, San Giovanni in Laterano.

Istanbul, Hippodrome.

The obelisk of Ramses II in Place de la Concorde.

London, Cleopatra's Needle.

NILE TO THE CITIES OF THE WORLD

Rome, Saint Peter's Square (above) and Piazza del Popolo (below).

Rome, Piazza dell'Esquilino (left).

Rome, Piazza di Montecitorio.

city that holds the world record for obelisks is Rome, with thirteen. The most spectacular of all is that now in Piazza del Popolo, originally raised by Ramses II in Heliopolis and brought to the Circus Maximus by Augustus. Alongside San Giovanni in Laterano is the obelisk of Thutmose III, brought from Thebes, and in Piazza di Montecitorio that built by Psammetichus II in Heliopolis.

Heliopolis is also the place of origin of the obelisk, carved with inscriptions relative to Ramses II, that now stands in front of the Pantheon in Piazza della Rotonda. Smooth, with no hieroglyphics at all, is instead the spire in Saint Peter's Square, erroneously attributed by Pliny the Elder to Sesostris' son.

Rome, Piazza del Quirinale.

CONTENTS